Tucholsky Wagner Zola Scott Sydow Freud Schlegel
Turgenev Fonatne Wallace
Twain Walther von der Vogelweide Fouqué Friedrich II. von Preußen
Weber Freiligrath Frey
Fechner Fichte Weiße Rose von Fallersleben Kant Ernst Frommel
Richthofen
Hölderlin
Engels Fielding Eichendorff Tacitus Dumas
Fehrs Faber Flaubert
Eliasberg Ebner Eschenbach
Feuerbach Maximilian I. von Habsburg Fock Zweig
Ewald Eliot Vergil
Goethe Elisabeth von Österreich London
Mendelssohn Balzac Shakespeare Dostojewski Ganghofer
Lichtenberg Rathenau Doyle Gjellerup
Trackl Stevenson Hambruch
Mommsen Tolstoi Lenz Droste-Hülshoff
Thoma Hanrieder
von Arnim Hägele Hauff Humboldt
Dach Verne
Reuter Rousseau Hagen Hauptmann Gautier
Karrillon Garschin
Defoe Baudelaire
Damaschke Hebbel
Descartes
Hegel Kussmaul Herder
Wolfram von Eschenbach Schopenhauer Rilke George
Darwin Dickens Grimm Jerome
Bronner Melville Bebel
Campe Horváth Aristoteles Proust
Voltaire Federer
Bismarck Vigny Barlach Herodot
Gengenbach Heine
Storm Casanova Tersteegen Grillparzer Georgy
Chamberlain Lessing Langbein Gilm
Brentano Lafontaine Gryphius
Strachwitz Claudius Schiller Kralik Iffland Sokrates
Katharina II. von Rußland Bellamy Schilling
Gerstäcker Raabe Gibbon Tschechow
Löns Hesse Hoffmann Gogol Wilde Vulpius
Gleim
Luther Heym Hofmannsthal Morgenstern
Roth Klee Hölty Goedicke
Heyse Klopstock Kleist
Luxemburg Puschkin Homer Mörike
Machiavelli La Roche Horaz Musil
Navarra Aurel Musset Kierkegaard Kraft Kraus
Lamprecht Kind Hugo Moltke
Nestroy Marie de France Kirchhoff
Laotse Ipsen Liebknecht
Nietzsche Nansen Ringelnatz
Marx Lassalle Gorki Klett Leibniz
von Ossietzky May
vom Stein Lawrence Irving
Petalozzi Knigge
Platon Pückler Michelangelo Kafka
Sachs Poe Kock
Liebermann Korolenko
de Sade Praetorius Mistral Zetkin

The publishing house tredition has created the series **TREDITION CLASSICS**. It contains classical literature works from over two thousand years. Most of these titles have been out of print and off the bookstore shelves for decades.

The book series is intended to preserve the cultural legacy and to promote the timeless works of classical literature. As a reader of a **TREDITION CLASSICS** book, the reader supports the mission to save many of the amazing works of world literature from oblivion.

The symbol of **TREDITION CLASSICS** is Johannes Gutenberg (1400 – 1468), the inventor of movable type printing.

With the series, tredition intends to make thousands of international literature classics available in printed format again – worldwide.

All books are available at book retailers worldwide in paperback and in hardcover. For more information please visit: www.tredition.com

tredition was established in 2006 by Sandra Latusseck and Soenke Schulz. Based in Hamburg, Germany, tredition offers publishing solutions to authors and publishing houses, combined with worldwide distribution of printed and digital book content. tredition is uniquely positioned to enable authors and publishing houses to create books on their own terms and without conventional manufacturing risks.

For more information please visit: www.tredition.com

# The Praise of a Godly Woman

Hannibal Gamon

# Imprint

This book is part of the TREDITION CLASSICS series.

Author: Hannibal Gamon
Cover design: toepferschumann, Berlin (Germany)

Publisher: tredition GmbH, Hamburg (Germany)
ISBN: 978-3-8495-0538-7

www.tredition.com
www.tredition.de

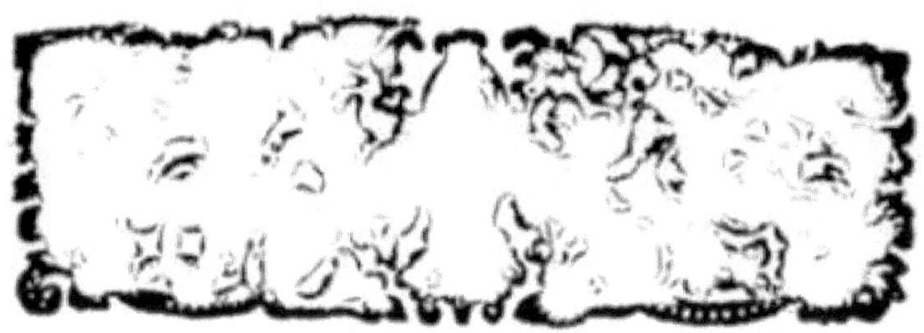

# TO THE TRVLY

NOBLE Iohn Roberts,
Son and Heire to the Right
Honourable Richard *Lord* Roberts
of *Truro*: the Vnualuable Riches of
ſincere Grace here, and of Eternall
Glory hereafter.

Honovrable Sir,

Although it bee true (which a worthy
Diuine [1] obferueth) that formall Hypocrites are heartned and
hardned in their lewd courfes & falfe conceits of happineffe, when
they heare more infamous Sinners than themfelues, glorioufly and
flatteringly commended at their Deaths; yet we Image need not
feare any fuch bad effect by the Funerall-commendation of Gods
true Saints; becaufe the publike Teftimonie of their iuft Praifes doth
not onely make the wicked more inexcufable, and the Glory of Gods
Graces fhine farre brighter to Pofteritie; but alfo enkindleth in the
hearts of the godly a greater fire of Zeale for imitation. Thefe are
fome of the Ends, why it hath euer been and is ftill an vnreproueable Cuftome in Gods Church, that the Godly fhould be *Marked* [2]
and *Honoured* [3] at their Deaths, as *Hezekiah* was by all *Iudah* &
*Ierufalem: Valentinean, Satyrus* and *Theodofius* by Saint *Ambrofe* [4]:
*Bafil, Gregory* and *Gorgonia* by *Nazianzen* [5]: *Nepotian, Paula* and
*Marcella* by *S. Ierom* [6]. Had not their Holy Liues and Happie
Deaths beene publifhed by fuch vnpartiall Pens, wee fhould haue
bin ignorant now of many excellent Courfes of fanctified Men and
Women, of many comfortable workings of the Holy Ghoft in them,
and fhould haue wanted many inflaming Motiues to follow their
religious fteps. Vpon this confideration I was bold to commend vnto
Gods people the more Image than Ordinary paffages of your Honourable Mothers Holy Life and Death: wherein I haue as a Chriftian
fpoken the truth of a Chriftian, that is, (as Saint *Ierom* [7] protefteth
in a like cafe) made a true Narration; not a Vain-glorious Panegyr-
ick. Let Poets and Oratours praife thofe women, which *Poppæa*-like
[8], are graced with all other things fauing a Gracious Heart: Let
them commend their Wit, Wealth, Beautie, Nobilitie, and other Gifts

of Fortune (as they call them) in ſtead of Vertues [9]. Wee the Miniſters of Chriſt, and Stewards of the Myſteries of God, muſt adorne
none with the Honourable Attributes of Heauenly Praiſe; but ſuch
as are truly beautified, enriched, and ennobled with the Purity and
Power of Gods Feare in their Humble Soules [10]. This praiſe the
Lord will Proſper [11], which is vttered in that *Wiſdome* [12], whereof the *Feare of the Lord is the beginning.* But for the Saints themſelues:
I dare ſay with Saint *Auguſtine* [13], that they deſire more the Imitation, than the Commendation Image of their vertues: and therefore
to tell you the truth (as the ſame Father doth his friend) you ſhould
neuer haue heard mee commend this deceaſed Lady, but in hope,
that Gods Graces in Her might by this meanes, ſuruiue in your religious Imitation, and not only in you and all them that are of Her
bloud; but alſo in all them that haue heard or ſhall reade this Ser-
mon. This is all the gaine I looke and pray for, that Gods [14] word,
which I haue faithfully alledged (not without ſome Illuſtrations (I
confeſſe) borrowed from the holy Fathers [15], whereof I need not to
be aſhamed) may be conſtantly practiſed by vs all. For when all is
done and ſaid, aſſure your ſelfe (Deare Sir) it is only the Life of
Grace, the Grace of the *Feare of the Lord* can truly Honour you, or
any vpon earth, ſweetly comfort you at your Death, and eternally
Glorifie your Soule and Bodie in Heauen. Abandon then I beſeech
you in the name of Chriſt [16], all iniquitie, and all workers of iniquitie, yea abominate the ſweeteſt ſin, to which your youthfull affections are moſt endeared, elſe you will neuer be able to encline and
enlarge Image them to the purſuit and practiſe of ſo excellent and
Glorious a Grace as the *Feare of the Lord;* becauſe this godly Feare
and the impenitent Allowance of any luſt, is as incompatible as
Heauen and Hell: ſo that if you ſhould hate to be diuorced from
your Boſome-ſin whatſoeuer it be (which God forbid) you could
haue no true right and intereſt to the precious promiſes of this and
of that other life [17]. Thinke on this continually, and hold it your
greateſt Honour, the Nobleſt imployment of your Soule, as it is indeed, to keep your ſelfe (as a King [18] did before you.) from your
iniquitie. *Quod ſi tu (quod procul abſit) nolueris, ego liber ero. Epiſtola,
immo concio me hæc mea, cum lecta fuerit, abſoluet.* [19] And ſo I reſt,
being mindfull of your Vertues,

*Yours in all Chriſtian Deuotion,*
*and heartieſt prayer to*
*God for you,*

Hannibal Gamon.

# FOOTNOTES:

[1] M^r. *Bolter* Difc. of true Happineffe, p. 61.

[2] *Pfalm. 37. 37. Deut. 34. 7, 10, 11, 12. Hebr. 3. 2. & 11. cap.*

[3] *2 Chron. 32. 33.*

[4] *S. Ambr. tom. 3.*

[5] *Greg. Nazian. Orat. 30. Orat. 28. Orat. 25.*

[6] *S. Ierom. Ad Heliod. Ad Euftoch. Ad Princip. Ad Ocean.*

[7] *Teftor Iesum cui illa feruiuit & ego feruire cupio, me utramq, in partē nihil fingere; fed quafi Chriftianū de Chriftianâ quæ funt vera proferre, id eft, Hiftoriam fcribere non Panegyricum. S. Ierom, Epitaph. Paulæ.*

[8] *Poppæa cuncta alia fuêre præter Honeftum animum. Tacit. Annal. l. 13.*

[9] *Laudauit ipfe Nero apud roftra formam eius & quòd diuinæ formæ parens fuiffet, aliaque fortunæ munera pro Virtutibus. Id. Annal. l. 16.*

[10] *Efai. 61. 3.*

[11] *Ecclef. 15. 10.*

[12] *Prou. 9. 10.*

[13] *Epift. 125.* where S. *Auguftine* refufeth to commend vnto a wicked Husbād his godly wife that was dead, not onely becaufe fhe defired not his praife, faying: *Laudem ab hominibus iam illa non quærit, imitationem verò tuā tantum quærit etiam defuncta, quantum te dilexit etiam diffimilem viua;* but alfo becaufe her Husband loued Her not, which he proueth thus: *Nam utiq fi amares, cum illa effe poft mortem defiderares, quod profectò non eris, fi quàlis es, talis eris.*

[14] *Ier. 23. 22, 28. 1 Pet. 4. 11. Tit. 2. 8. 2 Tim. 2. 15. 1 Tim. 4. 13. & 6. 3.*

[15] *— Ingenuo pudore qui ornabat ætatem, quid cuius effet, confiteri … Illud (aiebat) Tertulliani, iftud Cypriani, hoc Lactantij, illud Hilarij eft. Sic Minutius Fœlix, ita Victorinus, in hunc modum eft locutus Arnobius. S. Ierom. ad Heliodor de Nepotian.*

[16] 2 *Theſſ.* 3. 6. 2 *Tim.* 2. 19. *Prou.* 4. 14. 1 *Cor.* 5. 11. *Epheſ.* 5. 11. *Pſalm.* 26. 4, 5. & 119. 32, 36, 128. 2 *Chron.* 19. 2. & 20. 37.

## THE PRAISE OF A
Godly Woman.

Prov. 31. 30.

*— But a woman that feareth the Lord, ſhee ſhall be praiſed.*

Praiſe is a Debt (ſaith *Gregory Nazian-zen* [20] ) and it muſt be paid, not to men alone, but to women alſo; yet not to euery woman, be ſhee neuer ſo noble, wittie, wealthy or faire [21], vnleſſe ſhe be godly withall: For *fauour is deceitfull, and beautie is vaine; but a woman that feareth the Lord, ſhee ſhall be praiſed.*

The Diuiſion.

A promiſe this is and affirmatiue, and an affirmatiue promiſe hath two parts in it. The firſt is the Partie to whom it is made, and ſhee is *Muliertimens [Pg 2] Dominum. A woman that feareth the Lord,* which is alſo the reaſon why ſhe ſhall be praiſed: euen becauſe ſhe is *a woman fearing the Lord.* The ſecond is the thing promiſed, and that is *Lauda-bitur, ſhe ſhall be praiſed.*

# FOOTNOTES:

[17] *1 Tim. 4. 8.*

[18] *Pſal. 18. 23.*

[19] *S. Ierom. ad Caſtorin. Materteram.*

[20] *Orat. 25. fol. 439. Rom. 13. 7, 8.*

[21] *Non poſſumus reprehendere diuini artificis opus; ſed quem delectat corporis pulchritudo, multo magis illa delectet venuſtus, quæ ad imaginem, Dei eſt intus, non foris comptior. S. Ambr. Inſtit. Virg. c. 4. Prou. 11. 22. Eccle. 11. 2. ... Homo igitur mihi non tam vultu quam affectu admirand*ˢ *emineat atque excellat: vt in his laudatur, in quibus etiam Deus prophetico iudicio laudatur de quo ſcriptum eſt Pſal. 66. 5. Terribilis in conſiliis ſuper filios hominum; cuius opera coram Deo luceant, qui bona iugibus operibus facta contexat. Id. ib. cap. 3.*

I.

In the former, it is not enough that ſhe is a woman, becauſe euery woman is not *Timens*, one that *Feareth*, nor ſufficient that ſhe *Feareth*; becauſe euery woman that feareth is not *Timens Dominum*, one *that feareth the Lord*; but *ſhe* that *ſhall be praiſed*, is all three. 1. A woman by nature [22], where the weaker her ſex is, the more ſhee ſhall be commended. 2. By Grace [23], *a woman that feareth*, where the continuall act of this Fearing is required. 3. *That feareth the Lord*, where the right Obiect of her continuall feare is limited.

II.

And in the latter we are to conſider; Firſt, to what matters, *Laudabitur*, her praiſe will reach, and in what reſpect to *Ipſa* Her perſon. Then ſecondly, When *ſhe ſhall be praiſed*; not for the preſent, perhaps, no more than ſhe hath beene heretofore; yet *Laudabitur*, the time will come when *ſhe ſhall be praiſed*, and then too her praiſe ſhall ſo be, that it ſhall be ſtill. Thirdly, of whom ſhee ſhall haue praiſe, for *Laudabitur* is an action, and must bee done of ſome agent, therefore we muſt finde who ſhal praiſe her, and they will fall out to be her Huſband and her Children (if ſhe haue them [24]) and if they faile in this dutie, then the godly ſhall praiſe her; and if they ceaſe to doe it, then her own [Pg 3] workes ſhall praiſe her, yea rather than faile, God

himſelfe ſhall praiſe her, which is beſt of all. So ſure ſhe is to be
praiſed, not for the preſent onely, but for euer. And ſo this Text beſides that it is a *Promiſe*, it is alſo a *Motiue* to ſtirre vs vp to feare God,
that so we also may haue true and eternall praiſe of God. It is both,
and both waies wee to haue vſe of it, as of a *Promiſe*, and as of a
*Motiue*: both theſe waies at once; *A woman that feareth the Lord ſhe
ſhall be praiſed.*

# FOOTNOTES:

[22] *Naturale vocabulū eſt Fœmina. naturalis vocabuli generale, Mulier. – Tert. de Virg. Veland. cap 4.*

[23] *Aliud eſt Timere ſimpliciter, aliud Timere Deum – – quippe timere & amare ſimpliciter prolata, affectione: cuᵐ additamento aute virtutes ſignificāt. Simplices nempe affectiones inſunt naturaliter nobis tanquam ex nobis, Additamenta ex Gratiâ. S. Bern. de Grat. & lib. Arb.*

[24] *Mulier enim no naturâ nomcn cſt vxoris, ſed vxor coditione nomen eſt mulieris. Tert. ib. c. 5. Gen. 2. 23. Hæc vocabitur mulier, quoniam de viro ſuo ſumpta eſt: Quia ſumpta eſt (inquit) de viro suo, non quia virum experta ... Non enim corruptelæ, ſed ſexus vocabulum eſt. Gal. 4. 4. Luke 1. 28. S. Ambr. ibid. c. 5.*

A Promiſe, and Motiue.
I.
*The partie that ſhall be praiſed.*

A weake ſex [25] to beginne with, and yet being ſtrengthned by Grace [26], no impediment; but that a woman as wel as a man may feare the Lord, and haue praiſe of him, and ſo become the partie who ſhall, and one Reaſon too, why *ſhee ſhall he praiſed.*

For a woman muſt be more good than nature, art, policie, preferment can make her, elſe ſhee is not good enough for Gods Spirit to praiſe her. He commends neither men nor women conſidered in their pure Naturalls only, in that eſtate of corruption, they all heare alike to their diſgrace, that they are *All vnder ſinne [27], All come [28] ſhort of the glory of God,* and are *All the children of [29] wrath,* becauſe they *Are without all feare of God* [30]

By nature then both ſexes are alike faultie, alike diſcōmendable in Gods ſight, and ſo they ſhould be in ours. We ſhould not diſpraiſe women more than men, for the ſex ſake only (as ſome doe [31]) becauſe they haue as noble ſoules as men, for [32] ſoules haue no ſexes, (as Saint *Ambroſe* ſaith) nor praiſe women for the endowments of the fleſh onely (as [Pg 4] otherſome doe [33]) vnleſſe they be adorned alſo with the ſauing Graces of the Spirit, whereof a chiefe one is not noble birth, great wealth, excellent wit, or rare beautie: but *the feare of the Lord,* his treaſure. [34] This godly feare is that, that makes a

Woman in relation [35] to God, praiſe-worthy. And good reaſon it
ſhould do ſo, if we regard the weakneſſe of a woman, in whom ſo
excellent a Grace as *the feare of the Lord*, is found, and the Nobleneſſe
of fearing the Lord, being ſo found.

# FOOTNOTES:

[25] *1 Pet. 3. 7. Ier. 50. 37. Nah. 3. 13. Gal. 3. 27, 28.*

[26] *— Ex parte natura (niſi ſit fortitude maioris gratiæ) faciliùs incarnatur ad malum ſexus formineus. Bonau. L. 2. d. 21. q. 3. p. 18.*

[27] *Rom. 3. 9.*

[28] *Rom. 3. 23.*

[29] *Epheſ. 2. 3.*

[30] *Rom. 3. 18.*

[31] *Eurip. Plutarc. de Tranquilit Mulier quantibuis proba, Mulier tamen eſt.*

[32] *Anima enim ſexum non habet. — De Virg. som. 1. lib: 3. fol. 99.*

Firſt, a womans weakneſſe is naturally [36] greater than the mans, and therefore by how much her fleſh is weaker, and her ſpirit leſſe willing, by ſo much the combate ſhe hath, is more difficult, and the victory ſhe gets, more commendable. I know a man (*Bleſenſis* by name) that thought two things ſhould excuſe him at the dreadfull day of iudgement, the Frailty of his fleſh, and the Ignorance of his minde; but then he feared leſt God would iudge men by womē, whoſe ſex being more fraile, more ignorant than that of mens, were for all that oftentimes more holy, more deuout than many men.

Secondly, the *Feare of the Lord* is the trueſt Nobilitie (as *Gerſon* [37] proues) the nobleſt grace that can ennoble and extoll a man or a woman. Other naturall, ciuill, and meerely morall excellencies, perfections, and endowments a woman may haue, nay (which is neereſt the point) other kindes of Feare ſhe may haue, and yet be baſe, ſeruile, curſed as *Iezebel* [38], not praiſe-worthy, as namely, if ſhe feare men [39], or what elſe beſides more than [Pg 5] God, or not for God (as Saint *Bernard* [40] limits) or if ſhee feare God as a Iudge, in reſpect of his puniſhments only [41], & not as a Father for loue of his goodneſſe, and from an hatred of wickedneſſe, or if ſhe haue caſt off the feare of the Lord, which ſhee hath ſeemed to haue, or if ſhee puts off his *Feare* from time to time, and continues not in it.

# FOOTNOTES:

[33] *Cornel. Agrip. de Nobilit. fœminei fexus. Bocacius de claris muli-eribus.*

[34] *Ef. 33. 6.*

[35] *Caiet. in. loc.*

[36] *Naturaliter etiam maior lucti eft inter carnem et fpiritū mulieris quam viri: quantò enim caro eius infirmior, & fpiritus minus promptus, tãtò pugna difficilior – & victoria commēdabilior. Pet. Blef. fer. 33. p. 420. Timeo autem ne fortè viri à virginibus iudicentur: Comparatione tamē non Auctoritate: quia per duo tantum fcilicet: per Fragilitatē carnis & Igno-rantiam mentis putobã, &c. fer. 35. p. 428.*

[37] *Tractat. de Nobilitate, part. 2. p. 52. lit. E. Et Greg. Naz. Orat. 13. tom. I. fol. 352.*

[38] *2 Kings 9. 34. Act. 14. 25. 1 Ioh. 4. 18.*

[39] *Matth. 10. 28. Ef. 51. 12.*

Looke we then firft to the Obiect of the *Laudable womans feare*, that he whom fhe feareth be the Lord, in refpect of his Mercy and Iuftice both; then to the continuall employment of her *Feare*, not one that hath feared him, or will feare him; but one that doth feare him for the prefent, and continueth therein, elfe fhee is not a woman *Timens Dominum, Fearing the Lord*, and fo not worthy to be *praifed*.

I.
*The Obiect of her feare.*

Firft then (that the Obiect may be right) the [42] *Lord is her feare*, who fhal be praifed. For if He be not, all exquifiteneffes befides are nothing in comparifon; and if He be, all fufficiencies (remarkable in that fex) are improued, and all Duties (obferueable in the feare of the Lord) are practifed. To fee this the better, let vs follow *Tertullians* [43] rule, and oppofe one againft another, a veffel of difhonour againft a veffel of honour, a woman not Fearing, againft a woman Fearing the Lord.

*A womã fearleffe of God.*

She that fears not the Lord, ſets light by Gods anger and her Huſbands [44], not caring whether they bee pleaſed or diſpleaſed. Shee neglects to plant the feare of the Lord in her childrens hearts, [Pg 6] chuſing rather to be an example of wickedneſſe vnto them, and to miſplace them in mariage for ſiniſter reſpects. She brings want of things neceſſary to her family by her waſtefulneſſe, brauery, and idleneſſe. She contemnes her naturall and legall kindred, lifts vp her ſelfe aboue her equalls, diſdaines her inferiours, diſhonours her place by an ouer-loftie or an ouer-baſe and contemptible behauiour in the ſame. She alienates the hearts of Gods people from her, by neglecting the offices of courteſies and helpfulneſſe. She declines and vnderualewes the moſt ſearching meanes of Saluation, the Word, Prayer, Conference, Repentance, Meditation, Sacraments; in a word (according to Saint *Ambroſes* [45] Diſtinction) ſhe feares hell torments, becauſe ſhee hath ſinned, but ſhee feares not Gods diſpleaſure, leſt ſhe ſhould ſinne, and therefore ſhee liues and dies in worldlineſſe, wantonneſſe, pride, hatred, variance, emulations, wrath, ſtrife, reuenge, impatiencie, gluttonie, or ſome ſuch darling ſinne: and tell me (Beloued) if ſuch a woman not beautified and adorned with religion and the feare of the Lord, be worthy to bee praiſed of the Lord? I am ſure the ancient Fathers [46] declaime bitterly againſt her filthy heart, falſe haire, adulterate paintings, naked breaſts, new-fangled faſhions of ſuperfluous, monſtrous attire: & the holy Scriptures [47] vilifie her to her face, threatning her (notwithſtanding all her other ornaments [Pg 7] and excellencies of nature, art, policie, preferment,) that without this *Feare of the Lord, it ſhall not be well with her, Eccleſ. 8. 13. The Lord will come neare to her to iudgement, he will be a ſwift witneſſe againſt her, Mal. 3. 5. She ſhall leaue her memorie to be curſed [48], and her reproach ſhall not be blotted out, ſhe ſhall be counted vngodly of all [49], more bitter than death [50]. As rottenneſſe in her husbands bones [51], As ſpittle [52], yea As a Dogge [53],* and at laſt ſhe ſhall be caſt into hell fire, *Saluâ Veniâ,* without pardon from God, becauſe (ſaith *Tertullian* [54]) ſhe hath ſinned *Saluo metû,* without any feare of God.

# FOOTNOTES:

[40] *Convertatur ad ipſum etiam Timor tuus, quia peruerſus eſt timor omnis, quo metuis aliquid præter eum aut non propter eum. S. Ber. in cap. Ieiun. ſer. 2.*

[41] *Quid magnū eſt, pœnā timere? Quis enim nō timet? quis Latro, quis ſceleratus, quis nefarius? &c. S. Auguſt. de Verb. Apoſt. ſer. 15. fol. 332. tom. 10.*

[42] *Deut. 10. 12. 2 King. 17. 36. Luk. 12. 5. Eſ. 8. 13. Mal. 1. 6.*

[43] *Loquacitas in ædificatione nulla turpis, ſi quando turpis. Itaque ſi de aliquo bono ſermo eſt, res poſtulat contrarium quoque boni recenſere. Quid enim ſectandum ſit, magis illummabis, ſi quod vitandū ſit, proinde digeſſeris. Tertul. de Patien. c. 5. tom. 2.*

[44] *Esth. 1. 12, 17, 20, 22. Eccl. 26. 26. Eſ. 36. 9. & 3. 16. Prou. 30. 33. Eccleſ. 25. 13. & alibi paſſim. Vbi verò timor Dei non eſt, ibi diſſolutio vitæ eſt. S. Aug. de Temp. ſer. 213. tom. 10.*

[45] *Aliud eſt timere quia peccaueris, aliud timere ne pecces. Et ibi eſt formido de ſupplicio, hic ſolicitudo de præmio. Epiſt. 84. tum. 3. Eſt quem timor Dei ligat, qui non expaueſcit ad vultus hominū, ſed ad memoriam gehennalium tormentorum. Et hic quidem peccare non metuit, ſed ardere. S. Bern. de Tripl. Coberent: Vincul. &c. Eſ. 33. 14.*

[46] *Tertul. de Habit. Mulieb. & de Cultu Fœm. tom. 2. S. Cyprian de Diſcipl. & Hab. Virg. to. 2. Greg. Naz. aduerſ. mulier: Ambitiosè ſe or-nantes. to. 2. S. Ephræm aduerſ. improbas mulieres tom. 1. if his workes. Riuet. l. 3. c. 21.*

[47] *2 King. 9. 20, 30, 34. Eſ. 3. 16, &c. & 32. 9, 10, 11. 1 Pet. 3. 3, 4. Matth. 5. 36. & 6. 27. Eccleſ. 25. 13, 19.*

*A womā fearing the Lord.*

But on the other ſide what perſonall ſufficiency, what ſingular du-ty is there requiſite in a Woman, either in reſpect of God, or of her huſband, children, kindred, ſeruants, place, and of Gods people, which the life of Grace, the Grace of the Feare of the Lord doth not animate, aduance, and accompliſh? This godly Feare ennobleth Nobilitie, beautifieth Beautie, enricheth wealth, teacheth wit, wiſ-dome. She that hath this *Feare*, dare not for her heart, but be loath to offend her hufband, and deny her inferiority [55], but be an example of godlineffe to her children [56], prouide things neceffary for her feruants [57] both in health and in fickneffe; loue her naturall and legall [58] kindred, efteeme her equals aboue her felfe [59], countenance and relieue her inferiours [60], maintaine the dignitie of her place by all fuch vertues as may difcharge the [61] fame; winne the affections of Gods people, to her more and more, by the offices [62] of courtefies, falutations, gifts, vifitations, inuitations [Pg 8] and of helpfulneffe; yea fhe that feares God, dare not for her heart but *Honour them that feare God, Pfal. 15. 4.* but keepe her fet taskes [63] of hearing, reading, fafting, praying, meditating, moderating paffionate diftempers, and of all other gracious exercifes, of Selfe-deniall [64]; fo that there is not any knowne [65] finne which fhe nourifheth, alloweth, or goeth on in, but quaketh and trembleth at the very firft thoughts, yea motions and inclinations thereunto, as being in the fight [66] of an inuifible God, vnder the perpetuall prefence of his All-feeing glorious pure eye, which fhee will not prouoke to anger by any finne, for all the gold that euer the Sunne made, or fhall make while it ftands in Heauen [67].

# FOOTNOTES:

[48] *Eccleſ. 23. 26. Prou. 10. 7.*

[49] *Eccleſ. 26. 25.*

[50] *Eccleſ. 7. 26*

[51] *Prou. 12. 4.*

[52] *Eccleſ. 26. 21.*

[53] *Eccleſ. 26. 25.*

[54] *Sic ergò & ipſi, faluâ veniâ in gehennam detrudentur, dum faluô metû peccant. De pænit. c. 5. Reuel. 21. 8. & 22. 15.*

[55] *Gen. 3. 16. Eph. 5. 23.33. 1 Cor. 7. 34.*

[56] *1 Tim. 5. 10. 2 Tim. 1. 5. & 3. 15. Tit. 2. 4. Deut. 6. 7.*

[57] *Prou. 31. 15, 21. Matth. 8. 6.*

[58] *1 Tim. 5. 4. Eſth. 2. 7, 10. & 4. 4. Ruth 4. 15. Exod. 18. 7.*

[59] *Phil. 2. 3. Rom. 12. 10, 16.*

[60] *Iam. 2. 1. 1 Tim. 6. 18.*

[61] *Titus 2. 3.*

[62] *Luk. 1. 45, 56. Prou. 1. 20 & 5. 20 Gal. 6. 10 1 Tim 5. 10 Iob 6. 14*

This glorious deſcription of a woman fearing the Lord, is not mine (Bleſſed Brethren) but the Scriptures, wherein I finde; 1. The cauſe of her Feare to be not Selfe-Loue [68], but the Loue of God; not the ſpirit of Bondage [69]; but the Spirit of Adoption: 2. The Obiect of her feare to be not the precepts of men [70], but the Commandements of God [71]: not his Threats only [72], but his Promiſes alſo [73]: not his Anger only againſt ſin [74], but his Mercy alſo in Chriſt [75]: not his Preſence only, as a Reuenging Iudge [76], but his Forbearance alſo as a louing Father [77]. 3. The workings of her Feare to be in the heat of temptations and afflictions, [Pg 9] not Deſpairing [78]; but Beleeuing the forgiueneſſe of her ſinnes, not Limiting God to the present danger; but [79]waiting for his mercy, not Diſtruſting his Prouidence; but hoping for Good [80]: not Murmuring againſt him; but praiſing Him, and praying vnto Him [81], yea

(which is the proper Act of her Feare) not Louing any ſin, but hating
and eſchewing all ſin [82], not out of a ſlauiſh terrour of puniſhment;
but chiefly becauſe it is Sinne, an Infinite euill; and becauſe an Infinite Good God, whom ſhe loueth (ſaith Saint *Auguſtine*) is offended
by it, though ſhe ſhould neuer goe to Hell-fire to be puniſhed for it
[83].

# FOOTNOTES:

[63] *Gal. 6. 9. Iam. 1. 19. 1 Tim. 4. 13. 1 Theſſ 5. 17. Luk. 2. 37. Epheſ. 4. 26. Phil. 4. 5. 1 Pet. 3. 4. Luk. 9. 23. & 14. 26.*

[64] *Pſal. 18. 23. & 77. 10. Gen. 39. 9. Prou. 16. 6. & 8. 13.*

[65] *Gen. 17. 1. Pſal. 6. 8. & 116. 9. Act. 10. 33. 2 Cor. 6. 17. Iob 34. 21. Prou. 15. 3. & 5. 22. 2 Chron. 16. 9 1 King. 17. 1. Magna eſt cautela peccati, Dei ſemper preſentiam timere. S. Aug. de Temp. tom. 212. tom. 10.*

[66] *Multum enim refrænat homines cōscientia, ſi credamus nos in cōſpectu Dei uiuere, ſi non, tantum quæ gerimus uideri deſuper, ſed etiam quæ cogitamus, aut loquimur, audiri a Deo putamus &c. Lact. de Irâ Dei. c.8.*

[67] *Eſ. 3. 8. 1 Cor. 3. 22. Pſalm. 119. 14.72. 127.162.*

[68] *2 Tim. 1. 7 & 3. 2.*

[69] *Rom. 8. 15.*

[70] *Eſ. 29. 13.*

[71] *Deut. 4. 10. Eſ. 66. 2. Eccl. 12. 13. Prou. 13. 13. Pſal. 119. 161.*

[72] *Pſal. 119. 120. & 52. 6.*

[73] *2 Cor. 7. 1. Heb. 4. 1. Pſal. 130. 4.*

[74] *Deut. 5. 9*

[75] *Hos. 3. 5. Pſal. 33. 18 & 130. 4.*

[76] *Ier. 5. 22. Act. 10. 2, 33.*

[77] *Mal. 1. 6. Oſ. 3. 5. Hebr. 12. 9.*

II.
*The continuance of her Feare.*

Laſtly, in the Scriptures I finde Perſeuerance or Conſtancie [84] to be euer an inſeperable Attendant vpon her Feare! For ſhe is not one that hath not yet taſted of this ſauing Grace, or elſe not continued in the ſame; but ſhe is a woman for the preſent, *Timens Dominum, Fearing the Lord.* You ſhall neuer finde Her otherwiſe, than (as God would haue her) *In the feare of the Lord all the day long, Prou. 23. Fearing and keeping his Commandements alwaies, Deut. 4. Doing her Hus-*

*band Good and not euill all the daies of her life*, verſe the 12. of this Chapter.

It is true indeed, as Feare is oppoſed to Diffidence, *Luke 1.* So ſhe ſerves God without a Diſtruſtfull Feare all the daies of her life; be-cauſe of Gods continuall preſence with Her [85], continuall mercy towards Her [86], continuall power [87] ouer [Pg 10] Her, in Strengthening, Helping, and Vpholding Her, *Eſai. 41. 10.* But yet as Feare is oppoſed to Negligence, ſo ſhe ſtill feares God, leſt ſhe ſhould be ſecure by reaſon of his Power which is inuincible [88]; of his Wiſ-dome, which is infallible [89]; of his Mercy, which is compaſſionate [90]; and of his Iuſtice, which is inflexible [91].

# FOOTNOTES:

[78] *Ier. 17. 17. Ecclef. 2. 8.*

[79] *Pfal. 33. 18. 20. Ecclef. 2. 7.*

[80] *Pfal. 115. 11. & 56. 3. Ecclef. 2. 9.*

[81] *1 Cor. 10. 10. Pfalm. 22. 23. Act. 10. 2.*

[82] *Exod. 20. 20. Ecclef. 15. 13. Prou. 8. 13. & 16. 6. 2 Tim. 1. 7. 1 Ioh. 4. 18. Hof. 3. 5. Pfal. 97. 10. Ier. 4. 18. & 2. 19.*

[83] *Verò-Chriftianus – proficiēdo perveniet ad talem animū, vt plus amet Dominum quàm timeat Gehēnam: vt etiamfi dicat illi Deus, vtere delicife carnalibus fempiternis & quantum potes; pecca, nec morieris, nec in Gehēnam mitteris, sed mecum tantummodo non eris; exhorrefcat et omninò non peccet, non iam vt in illud quod timebat non incidat, fed ne illum quem fic amat, offendat. De Catechiz. Rudib. cap. 27. tom. 4. fol. 912.*

[84] *Ierem. 32. 39, 40. Deut. 4. 10. Prou. 23. 17. & 14. 2. 1 Tim. 2. 15.*

[85] *Matth. 28. 20 Ef. 43. 1, 2.*

[86] *Ier. 14. 9. Lam. 3. 22, 23.*

[87] *2 Cor. 12. 9. Ef. 26. 4. & 45. 24. Psal. 121. & 35. 24. Rom. 8. 26.*

It is as true alfo (which *Gerfon* and others haue obferued [92]) that many times a Deuout Soule is fo difquieted with a flauifh Feare of the Aduerfary; that fhe feares left fhe hath not any true Feare of Gods Maieftie; but yet (*B. B.*) lay the *Pelagian* what hee can to the contrary, fuch is the Euerlaftingneffe of Gods Loue [93], Mercie [94], and Couenant [95], the Vnconquerableneffe of his Power [96], the Immortality of his Word [97], the Certaintie of his Promifes [98], the Efficacie of Chrifts Spirit [99]; Prayer [100], Merits [101], and of Faith in them [102]; yea fuch is the durable vigour of this fauing Grace of *the Feare of the Lord* [103], that being once rooted by God, (as Saint *Auguftine* vrgeth) it cannot be remoued; but through it we may per-feueringly adhere vnto God according to his promife: *I will put my Feare in their hearts, that they fhall not depart from me, Ier. 32. 40.* with *Pfal. 80. 17.* She then that truely hath this *Feare*, doth fo feare the Lord in [Pg 11] Loue, and loue him in feare [104], that as in the

midſt of Gods not Conſuming, but Conſummating Anger (for ſo
Saint *Auguſtine* [105] calls Gods Anger towards the Godly) ſhee can
ſee the yerning and relenting Bowels of a Compaſſionate Father, ſo
in the height of Satans Terrifying iniections, ſhe can ſhunne and
abhorre Gods Diſpleaſure [106], more than all other miſeries of Puniſhments, and therefore in what ſtate ſoeuer ſhe be of Conſolation or
Deſertion, ſhee is ſtill the ſame Woman, *Timens Dominum, Fearing the
Lord.*

# FOOTNOTES:

[88] *Matth. 10. 28. Deut. 28. 58.*

[89] *Esai. 29. 15, 16. Psal. 50. 21.*

[90] *Esai. 43. 25. & 63. 9. & 49. 13, 15.*

[91] *Esai. 42. 14.*

[92] *De diuersis tentat. Diaboli, part 3. M*ʳ *Greenham 5.* part, among his Rules for an Afflicted minde.

[93] *Esai. 54. 8, 9, 10. c. 49. 15. Ier. 31. 3. 36. c. 33. 20, 21. Ioh. 13. 1. Rom. 8. 38, 39. Mat. 12. 20. Esai. 42. 3.*

[94] *Psalm. 103. 17. 2 Sam. 7. 15.*

[95] *Psal. 89. 28, 34. Esai. 55. 3. c. 59. 21. Ier. 32. 40.*

[96] *Ioh. 10. 29. Iude versf. 24. 1 Pet. 1. 5. Esai. 26. 4. Psal. 80. 17. Manus Dei est ista, non nostra vt non discedamus à Deo, manus inquā eius est ista, qui dixit, Timorem meum dabo in cor eorū &c. S. Aug. de Bono perseuer. c. 7. to. 7. Ier. 32. 27.*

[97] *1 Pet. 1. 23. 1 Ioh. 3. 9.*

[98] *Ephes. 1. 13. Numb. 13. 19. Ios. 21. 45. 1 Ioh. 5. 10. Hebr. 7. 27. c. 11. 11. Rom. 4. 21. 1 Cor. 1. 9.*

[99] *Esai. 59. 21. Ephes. 1. 13, 14. c. 4. 30. Ioh. 14. 16, 17. 1 Ioh. 2. 27.*

[100] *Luke 22. 32. Ioh. 17. 15, 20. Rom. 8. 34. Hebr. 7. 25.*

[101] *1 Pet. 1. 2, 3, 4, 5. 1 Ioh. 5. 4, 18.*

[102] *1 Pet. 5. 9. Ephes. 6. 6. Matth. 16. 18.*

[103] *Ierem. 31. 40. Perseuerantiam enim promisit Deus, dicens: Timorem meum dabo in cor eorum vt à me non recedant. Quod quid est aliud quàm talis ac tantus erit Timor meus, quem dabo in cor eorum, vt mihi perseuerantèr adhæreant? Idem de Bono Perseuer. c. 2. tom. 7. Rom. 11. 29.*

Thus wee haue seene who she is, who *shall be praised*, lest we should praise Her vnawares, whom we should not praise. And now it were good we did thinke a little better on the Reason, why *she shall be praised*, euen because she is such *a woman fearing the Lord.*

For if any thing, ſo rare and excellent a Grace as the *Feare of the Lord* is, ſhould moue vs to affect it, and labour for it, eſpecially being found in so weake a Veſſell as a Woman is [107]. For I could tell you, there are more *Michals* [108] than *Abigails* [109], more *Iezebels* [110] than *Sarah's* [111], more proud *Vaſthy's* [112], than humble *Eſthers* [113], more Fearefull women, than Women *Fearing the Lord*; and therefore the rarer ſuch Phœnixes are (as S. *Ierom* calls them [114]) not *One* to be found by wiſeſt *Salomon* [115], among a *Thouſand*, greater is her praiſe *that feareth the Lord* [116]. [Pg 12]

# FOOTNOTES:

[104] *Abſit enim vt timore pereat amor, ſi caſtus eſt timor. S. Aug. in Pſal. 119. tom. 8.*

[105] *Eſt ira conſummationis, & eſt ira cōſumptionis, (nam omnis Vindicta Dei, Ira dicitur) ſed aliquando ad hoc vindicat Deus, vt perficiat: aliquando ad hoc vindicat, vt damnet. Idem in Pſal. 58 to. 8. ſ. 599.*

[106] *– – Qui glutine Deo conglutinatur, id eſt charitate ... terribilius & horribilius ipsâ Gehenna iudicat, in re leuiſſima vultū omnipotentis scientèr offendere. S. Bern. de Tripl. Coharen. Vincul.*

[107] *1 Pet, 3. 7. Vir itaq, nominatus eſt, quòd maior in eo Vis eſt quàm in fœmina, & hinc Virtus nomen accepit. Item Mulier à mollicie eſt dicta ... velut Mollier. Lact. de Opſ. Dei. cap. 12.*

[108] *1 Sam. 18. 21. & 25. 41.*

[109] *2 Sam. 6. 16, 20.*

[110] *1 King. 21. 7. 2 King. 9. 22, 30.*

[111] *1 Pet. 3. 6.*

[112] *Eſth. 1. 12.*

[113] *Eſth. 8. 5.*

[114] *Optima fœmina rarior eſt Phœnice. Malarum fœminarū tam copioſa ſunt examina &c. S. Ier. epiſt.*

[115] *Ecclеſ. 7. 28. Prou. 3. 10.*

[116] *Laus tantò maior deferri ſolet, quantò eſt bonum rarius quod exigit Laudem. S. Aug. lib. 1. de Ciuit. Dei. cap. 28. tom. 5.*

Then I muſt tell you, that euery Feare is not commendable. Not that Feare which is Hypocriticall, for this is Superſtition, when men feare the Feare of Idolaters [117]. Not that feare which is Worldly, for this is wicked ſelfe-Loue, when men feare Men [118], Loſſe of Goods, Fire and faggot, more than God the Onely Soueraigne Commander of the Soule, the Only Dreadfull Threatner of euerlaſting Burnings. Nor that feare which is Seruile [119] or adulterate [120], for this is no Vertue (proues *Pariſ.*) when men feare the *Euill of Puniſhment* only; not the *Euill of Sinne,* as an Adultereſſe feares the

Comming home of her Hufband; but feares not the Committing of
Adultery. Nor is that feare commendable, which is Diftruftfull or
Immoderate like *Ruben* (as *Gerfon* [121] alludes) growen great, and
lying with *Bilhah*, for this is Infidelitie when men tie Gods Grace to
prefent deliuerance out of danger, without a Beleeuing and waiting
Spirit for his Mercie, *Efai. 28. 16.*

But the *Feare* for which a *Woman fhall be praifed*, is informed by
Wifdome, inftructed by Vnderftanding, directed by Counfell,
ftrengthned by Might, gouerned by Knowledge, adorned with Pie-
tie, as Saint *Ambrofe* collects out of the eleuenth of *Efay* [122]. It is a
Faithfull feare trufting in [Pg 13] God [123], and making Him her
*Feare, Efai. 8. 13.* and her Hope too in the Day of Euill, not without
this feruent Prayer vnto Him then: *Be not thou a Terrour vnto me, Ier.
17. 17.* A chaft and *Cleane Feare [124], Cleanfing from all filthineffe of
the flefh and Spirit.* [125] A Reuerent and Godly Fear [126], Preparing
the heart, Humbling the Soule in Gods fight [127], Trembling at his
Word [128], not Difobeying it, Efchewing [129] euill, Working right-
eoufneffe and Giuing much almes [130]. A Bleffed Feare it is [131],
Bleffing them that haue it, Bleffing the Lord that giues it, Praifing
Him and faying: *That his Mercy endureth for euer* [132].

# FOOTNOTES:

[117] *Eſai. 8. 12 Col. 2. 20.*

[118] *2 Tim. 3. 2. Mat. 10. 28. Quis animæ Dominator, niſi Deus ſolus? Quis iste, niſi ignium comminator? ... Illi potius metum conſecandū &c. Tertul. aduerſ. Gnoſt. c. 9. tom. 3.*

[119] *Timor Seruilis nō eſt Virtus, quialicet mala declinari faciat: non tamen hoc ſacit benè, id eſt ſaudibitèr; immo ilitèr et brutalitèr, videlicet ſolo metæ feræ, ilu enim occupat animum & intentionam timentis, oraculos cordis ad ſolam pœnæ euaſionem habeat &c. Paris. de Virtutibus, fol. 81. lit. H. & Paludan. l. 3. d. 34. q. 3.*

[120] *— Coniun quæ adulterinum animū gerit, etiam ſi timòre viri non adulterium perpetrat: tamen quod deeſt aperi, ineſt voluntati, Caſta verò alitèr timet: nam & ipſa times virum; ſed caſtè. Deniq, timet illa, no vir infeſtus adueniat, ista ne offenſus abſcedat. S. Aug. epiſt. 120. c. 21. to. 2.*

[121] *Ruben violat Balamdum nimium grandis effectus eſt, quia timor ſi ſimius eſt, dum ſe cuſtodire nititur, format inutiles imaginationes, quibus ſe connoluens à ſalutaribus impeditur. Tract. 10. ſuper, Magnificat. part 3.*

[122] *Lege Eſaiam: vide quantia ſubiecerit timorem vt faceret irreprehenſibilum & bonum Timorem. Spiritus inquit Sapientia &c. Talle Timori Domini iſta & eſt irrationabilis & inſipiens Timor, vnus ex illis: Foris pugnæ, intus Timores. In Pſal. 118. Ser. 5. tom. 4.*

Laſtly, it is an Euerlaſting Feare, euer encreaſing [133], and *Enduring for euer* [134], though not in reſpect of the Act of Declination or eſchewing of ſinne [135], becauſe in Heauen there is no feare of ſinning [136]; yet in reſpect of the Act of Celebration or Reuerencing God, becauſe there the Saints doe nothing elſe; but ſtill Giue Glory to Him, and Worſhip Him with humble Acknowledgement of their owne Vnworthineſſe, *Pſal. 19. 9.* with *Reuel. 4. 10. 11.*

The Excellencie of Godly Feare.

Now (Honourable and Beloued) though I haue ſet nothing at all beſides this Heauenly Manna before your eyes; yet your full Soules muſt not Loath it. For if that only is to be praiſed which is excellent [137], then (by your leaue) I muſt ſtand ſomewhat longer vpon the

Excellencie of this *Feare*, before *a Woman* can be *praised* that hath it.
[Pg 14]

# FOOTNOTES:

[123] *Pfal. 115. 11. & 147. 11. Efai. 50. 10.*

[124] *Pfal. 19. 9*

[125] *2 Cor. 7. 1.*

[126] *Hebr. 12. 28.*

[127] *Ecclef. 2. 17. & 21. 6.*

[128] *Efai. 66. 2. Eccle. 2. 15.*

[129] *Iob 1. 1.*

[130] *Act. 10. 35, 2, 31. Ecclef. 25. 1.*

[131] *Pfal. 112. 1. & 128. 1.*

[132] Pfal. 135. 13. & 118. 4 & 22. 23.

[133] *1 King. 18. 3. 12. Tob. 14. 4.*

[134] *Pfal. 19. 9. Reuel. 7. 10, 11 & 19. 1, 3, 4, 5, 6.*

[135] *Bonau. lib. 3. d. 34. q. 3. p. 89. Tho. Aquin. II q. 79. a. II*

[136] *In cœlo, vbi non eft peccatum Gloria eft & perpetuu laus & in-defeffæ præconia. S. Ierom. ad Therdoram. Epitaph. Lucinij. Timorem Offenfa & Timorem Pœnæ. Gloria Timorem Patriæ propter coram imperfectionem nō paritur. In tuto enim erimus et â pœnæ et ab offenfa. Parif. de Virtutibus, lit. A. F.*

[137] *Laudare plus eft quàm probare & prædicare. Nam Laudamus id quod excellit &c. Aufo. Popma de Differen. Virt. l. 3.*

I demand then what doe you count Excellent? Riches, Honour, Life. Why, thefe are neuer well gotten, nor well kept; but by *the Feare of the Lord.* So faith *Salomon, By the feare of the Lord are Riches and Honour, and Life* [138]. Say what you will, it muft needs be an Excellent thing wherwith Chrift Iefus Himfelfe was Filled, and that was with *The Spirit of this Feare, Efai. 11. 2.* [139]. An excellent thing which God Himfelfe so earneftly defires to be ftill in vs, and that is this Feare. *O* (faith He) *that there were fuch an Heart in them, that they would feare me, and keepe my Commandements alwaies* [140], which is indeed the *whole Dutie of Man* [141]; without which (Saint *Bernard*

concludes) *Euery man is Nothing*. He is not a Man (reafons a Schoole-
man [142]) but the Shadow of a Man; becaufe He imployes not his
Soule to that noble End for which he had it, namely, to be fquared
and ruled *by the feare of the Lord*: without which no man can fo much
as Begin to be wife, becaufe this *Feare is the Beginning* [143] *of wifdome*, nor fo much as *Begin to Loue God*, becaufe this *Feare is the Beginning of the Loue of God* [144]. It is the *Salt* (alludes *Blefenfis*) that
muft be in euery *Sacrifice* [145], in euery *Worke we doe*, fo that there is
no *Seruing God*, no *Reioycing* in Him [146], no heartie *Repenting* [147],
no *Chaft Conuerfing* [148], no *Perfecting Holineffe* [149], no *Working out
our Saluation*, but with *Feare and Trembling* [150]; nay there is no
*Saluation*, no *Bleffedneffe* without *Continuing in this Feare* [151], *Prou.
28. 14.* Againe, is not that Excellent, that will make vs more Excellent than our Neighbours [152], [Pg 15] that will Exalt vs aboue
them, that will keepe our hearts from Hardning [153], our Houfes
from Ouerthrowing [154]? but nothing can doe this; but this *Feare of
the Lord*. This feare (faith *Parif.* [155]) can caufe a fpiritual Earth-
quake in a mans Heart, able to ouerthrow all the Deuils ftrongeft
holds, any [156] Bofome-finne, be it neuer fo pleafing and profitable,
by reafon of that Contrarietie and Oppofition [157] that is betweene
Lying in any Sweet Sinne, and Liuing in Gods Feare and Fauour, as
you may fee, *Leuit. 25. 36.*

# FOOTNOTES:

[138] *Prou. 22. 4. & 19. 23. Ecclef. 1. 11, 12. & 23. 27. & 40. 26, 27. & 10. 20, 22.*

[139] *Inter Laudes meas & illa eft eximia: quod ipfum Chriftum Dominū Apothecam, immo fontem Gratiarum omnium & Virtutum replere dictus fum &c. Parif. de Moribus, fol. 99. Lit. P.*

[140] *Deut. 5. 29.*

[141] *Ecclef. 12. 13. Deum time – Ergo fi hoc eft omnis Homo, abfq, hoc Nihil omnis Homo. Serm. 20. in Cant.*

[142] *Vfus enim humani animi pendet à Timore conspictus Diuini tanquam à primi regula. Caiet. in Ecclef. c. 8 13. v.*

[143] *Prou. 9. 10. Iob 28. 28.*

[144] *Ecclef. 25. 12.*

[145] *Leuit. 2. 13. Pet. Blef. fer. 36. p. 430.*

[146] *Pfal. 2. 11.*

[147] *2 Cor. 7. 11. Eccl. 21. 6.*

[148] *1 Pet. 3. 2.*

[149] *2 Cor. 7. 1.*

[150] *Philip. 2. 12.*

[151] *Ecclef. 2. 10. 1 Tim. 2. 15.*

Laftly, this is an Excellent Feare, becaufe it is *A fountaine of Life* [158]: wherefore? *To driue away Sinnes* [159], Sinnes which haue beene committed by Repentance (faith S. *Bernard*) and Sinnes whereto we are Tempted, by Refiftance [160]; and yet this is not all the Excellencie of this Feare: For it is *A fountaine of life* alfo: *To Caufe vs to finde fauour at our Deaths* [161]; and which is more, Such an Excellent Feare as will make vs *Not feare, nor be afraid* [162]. Whereupon Saint *Auguftine* [163] concludes for my purpofe: *Difcat timere, qui non vult timere: Difcat ad tempus effe Solicitus, qui femper vult effe fecurus.* Let him learn to feare, that would not feare: Let him be wary and cautelous for a time, that would be happie and fecure for euer.

*Tertullian* giues the [Pg 16] reaſon [164], because if *We feare to Offend*, by Fearing we will take heed, leſt we Offend, and by Taking heed, we ſhall be in ſafetie; otherwiſe if wee preſume and be not alwaies watchfull ouer our hearts leſt they offend, we cannot be *Saued* [165], *Ier. 4. 14. Qui ſolicitus eſt, is verè poterit eſſe ſecurus*: He that is not ouer-bold on his owne ſtrength [166]; but confident in Christ [167], and liues not ſecurely in the minion-delight of any knowne ſinne; but ſtands in ſuch continuall awe of Gods *Preſence, Precepts, Promiſes, Threats*, that he dare not ſo much as once make any offer of incurring his Diſpleaſure by the impenitent Allowance of any ſinne in his heart [168], and ſtudies to do euery Good worke as carefully, as if it were the Laſt he should doe in this World, and as exactly, as if his whole Saluation depended vpon it, ſuch a Man (in Ancient *Tertullians* iudgement [169]) may be truely ſecure of Perſeuering in Grace here; and of being Glorified hereafter [170], *1 Thess. 5. 15, 24*. Once more I haue done. Is not that an excellent thing that is for the Good of them that haue it, & of their children after them? Riches, Honour, Beautie, Policie, theſe and the like are not oftentimes ſo, as we ſee by woefull experience in *Nabal, Haman, Abſalom, Achitophel*; but *the feare of the Lord* is euer ſo, *for the Good of them that haue it, and for their children after them*, as the [Pg 17] Prophet ſaith, *Ier. 32. 39*. and God himſelfe before him, *Deut. 5. 29*.

# FOOTNOTES:

[152] *Prou. 12. 26. Ecclef. 15. 5.*

[153] *Prou. 28. 14.*

[154] *Ecclef. 27. 3.*

[155] *Ego fum Tempeftas ad liberationem & falutem, Terræmotum fpiritualem in corde humano faciens, et omnia Diabolica ædificia in co fubuertens et difcutiens ab codem. Parif. de Moribus fol.* 99. *lit. F.*

[156] *Prou. 8. 13. & 16. 6. Pfal. 119. 6, 36. 117. 128. v. Iam. 2. 10. Pfal. 86. 11.*

[157] *Sed aiunt quidā: Satis Deum habere fi corde & animo fufpiciatur, licet actu minus fiat. Itaq fe faluo metu et fide peccare; hoc eft Saluâ caftitate, matrimonia violare, Saluâ pietate, parēti venenum temperare.* Tertul. de *Pœnit. c. 5. tom. 2.*

[158] *Prou. 14. 27.*

[159] *Ecclef. 1. 21.*

[160] *Timor Domini expellit peccatum, fine quod iam admiffum eft, fine quod tentat intrare. Expellit fanè illud quidem pœnitende, hoc Refiftendo. Serm. de Diuerf. Affect.*

[161] *Ecclef. 1. 13.*

[162] *Ecclef. 34. 14. Exod. 20. 20. Prou. 1. 33. & 19. 23. Pfal. 27. 1, 2, 3. & 34. 4. — Auferendi funt metus, fed ita, vt hic folus relinquatur, qui quoniam legitimus ac verus eft, folus efficit, ut poffint cætera omnia non timeri, Lact. de Vero Cultu. l. 6. c. 17. Qui enim Deum veracitèr timet, nihil terrenum & caducum timet,immo ex ipfo Timore Dei, ipfis Timoribus fupereffertur. Bonau. lib. 3. d. 34. q. 1. p. 62.*

[163] *De Temp. Serm. 214. tom. 10.*

[164] *Nam qui præfumit, minus veretur, minus præcauet, plus periclitatur &c. De Cultu Fæm. cap. 2. & de Pænit. cap. 6. — Volo te timere & non timere, præfumere & non præfumere, timere vt pæniteas, non timere vt præfumas. Porro præfumere ne diffidas, non præfumere ne torpefcas. Ber. cp. 87. ad Oger.*

[165] *Prou. 4. 23. Ier. 4. 14, 18. & 16. 10, 11, 12. Eſ. 55. 7. Mat. 15. 19. Nec ſufficit non egiſſe aliquid impium, ſi mēte cogitatur impietas. S. Hilar. in Pſal. 65. fol. 424.*

[166] *Prou 28. 26. Rom. 7. 18. & 11. 20.*

[167] *Phil. 4. 13. 2 Tim. 2. 1. & 4. 18. Eph. 6. 10. 2 Chron. 16. 8, 9. et. 20. 12. Deut. 6. 3, 4. Quicquid eſt circa te vel in te unde poſſis præſumere, abjice à te, & tota præſumptio tua Deus ſit, illius indigens eſto, vt implearis &c. S. Aug. in Pſal. 85.*

[168] *Pſal. 66. 18. 1 Pet. 3. 15. Ez. 33. 31. Pſal. 24. 4 Iam. 4. 8. Heb. 10. 22. Redi ad te, intus tibi eſto iudex. Ecce in cubiculo tuo abſcondito, in ipſa vena intima cordis tui vbi tu ſolus es, & ille qui videt; illic tibi diſpliceat iniquitas, vt placeas Deo.... Parum eſt in vultù, parum est in lingua, in corde noli respicere, id eſt, noli diligere, noli acceptare. Idem in Pſal. 65. to 8.*

[169] *De cultu Fæm. cap. 2. to. 2.*

[170] *2 Theſſ. 3. 3. 2 Tim. 2. 19. Ioh. 15. 16. Luke 10. 20. Ioh. 16. 22. & 10. 28, 29. v. Pſal. 35. 5. & 125. 1. Prou. 10. 30.*

There is no want to them that haue this *Feare* of any Good thing that is Good for them [171]. For firſt, *Pſal. 25. 14. The ſecret, that is, the feare of the Lord, is with them that feare Him;* and is not that enough, though I ſhould ſay no more with the Pſalmiſt, becauſe *Godly Feare is Gods Treaſure, Eſai. 33. 6.* and *Better little with it* (ſaith *Salomon*) *than Great Treaſure* [172]? But there is more behind to moue you further to affect this Excellent Grace. For if you will *Feare the Lord,* He will ſhew you his *Couenant* [173] *of life and peace* [174], *Teach you the way that you ſhall chuſe* [175], *Haue a Booke of remembrance written before Him for you* [176]: *Hee will Ariſe vnto you the Sunne of Righteouſneſſe with healing in his wings* [177]: *He wil hide you in his preſence from the pride of men* [178], *Keepe you ſecretly in a Pauilion from the ſtrife of tongues, Deliuer you in Temptation euen againe* [179]; yea *He will take pleaſure in you* [180], *Pitie you as a Father doth his children* [181], *Fulfill your Deſire, Heare your crie and ſaue you* [182]. And what is all this, but in a word (the word of my Text) *Hee will praiſe you,* which is the Thing Promiſed to *a woman fearing the Lord.*

II.
*The thing promiſed.*

*In what re∫pect to* Ip∫a.

*Ip∫a Laudabitur: She ∫hall be prai∫ed.*

She ∫hall be ∫o; but may not that labour be ∫pared? For a man would thinke, ∫he hath been prai∫ed all this while; becau∫e Godly Feare, the Grace of God in Her, and the onely cau∫e of her Prai∫e, hath beene alreadie ∫o much commended vnto you? No (Beloued) my Text (you ∫ee) applies [Pg 18] and appropriates this prai∫e to *Ip∫a*, Her own Per∫on, by vertue indeed of *the Feare of the Lord*. For were it not for that, it were better Contemning Her, yea Contending [183] with Her, than Commending Her, becau∫e that is a con∫tant marke of the Godly to Contemne the vngodly, *P∫al. 15. 4.* This, of the wicked to Prai∫e the wicked, to Ble∫∫e the Couetous, whom *the Lord abhorreth, P∫al. 10. 3.* It is not her Friend∫hip, no nor *Carnis bona* (as Saint *Ierom* [184] calls them) *the Good endowments of the fle∫h*, can priuiledge him from a *Cur∫e*, if ∫o be, he prai∫e her without or aboue [185] her De∫erts, *Prou. 27. 14.* Onely *the feare of the Lord*, with the excellent fruits thereof, is Gods Gift [186], for which (∫aith *Fulgentius* [187]) ∫he ought, and he may ∫afely commend her, becau∫e then, not ∫hee; but *Gods Grace* in her is *Prai∫ed, Ephe∫. 1. 6.* Yea then, *not ∫he*, but *God him∫elfe is Glorified* in Her, *Gal. 1. 24.*

# FOOTNOTES:

[171] *Pſal. 34. 9, 10. Ecclef. 40. 26, 27. & 1. 16.*

[172] *Prou. 15. 16.*

[173] *Pſal. 25. 14.*

[174] *Mal. 2. 5.*

[175] *Pſal. 25. 12.*

[176] *Mal. 3. 16.*

[177] *Mal. 4. 2.*

[178] *Pſal. 31. 20, 21.*

[179] *Ecclef. 33. 1.*

[180] *Pſal. 147. 11.*

[181] *Pſalm. 103. 13. Mal. 3. 17.*

[182] *Pſal. 145. 19.*

But what? is not *She Praiſed*, when Her Huſband, Her Children, Her Kindred, Her Friends, Her Attendants, Her Wit, Her Wealth, Her Beautie, Her Nobilitie, or all theſe and the like of Hers are commended? Yes, all theſe come very neere Her, and mutually receiue luſtre and eminencie from this Godly Feare; but they are not *Ipſa*, Her ſelfe, that is, [188] principally Her Soule truely Generous, and ennobled with the *Feare of the Lord.* Vntill ſuch an Humble Soule be found in Her, She is not She, that *ſhall be adorned with the Garment of praiſe, Eſai. 61. 3.* Therefore Saint *Ierom* [189] [Pg 19] would not commend in Noble *Marcella* any thing ſaue Her owne Godly ſelfe. *Ipſa Laudabitur*: She is She that ſhall be Praiſed.

# FOOTNOTES:

[183] *Prou. 28. 4 & 24. 24. & 17. 15. Eccl. 10. 23, 29. Tho. Aquin. 22. q. 115. a. 2. Corp.*

[184] *Ego carnis bona quæ femper & ipfe contempfit, in animæ laudibus nō requiram − − ad Heliodor. Epitah. Nepot.*

[185] *Prou. 27. 14. Vox autem grandis, laus excedens menfurā Meritorum hîs intelligetur − Parif. de Moribus. fol. 123. lit. M.*

[186] *Ef. 26. 12. 1 Cor. 15. 10. & 12. 6. Phil. 2. 13. Ier. 32. 40.*

[187] *Laudari in bonis operibus debes; fed in eo quod operaris, hominū laudes expectare non debes − Deus Laudetur in operibus tuis. De ftatu Vidu. ad Gallam epift. 2. Si qua fane in Sanctis digna laude vel admiratione intueor, clará luce veritatis difcutiens, profectò reperio Laudabilem fiue Mirabilem alium apparere atque alium effe, & Laudo Deum in Sanctis eius. S. Bern. Ser. 13. in Cant.*

[188] *1 Pet. 3. 4. Enimverò quis non animæ dabit fummam omnem, cuius nomine totius Hominis mentio titulata eft. Tertul. de Anima. cap. 13.*

And fo we fee how far forth Praife is to be extended to Her. Now to fpeak of the Extent of Her Praife: Let the word haue his full latitude. *Laudabitur* is generall, no kinde is limited. 1. Therefore for the Extent, to be praifed euery manner of way. 2. For the Time when it fhall be beft for her. 3. For the Praifer, by him who can beft doe it. Of all thefe briefly.

I.
*What Praife fhe fhall haue. The Extent of Laudabitur.*

Firft, what praife fhe fhall haue. 1. Euen that (which being true) is euer accompanied with Deareft Loue to her perfon [190]. 2. Higheft eftimation of Gods abundant graces in Her [191]. 3. Frequent Commemoration of them [192]. 4. Moderate Lamentation at her Death [193]. 5. Solemne Funerals according to the Dignitie of her place [194]. 6. And aboue all, with precife imitation of her excellent Vertues [195]. All this Honour God allowes Her, that honours Him with His Feare [196]. But becaufe all Praife is properly in Words (as the Schoole-man teacheth [197]) and better words fhee cannot haue to praiſe Her, than God himſelfe ſpeakes [198], therefore ſhe ſhall be Commended in no other, neither in regard of God, nor of her Husband, Children, Kindred, Seruants, and Gods People.

Firſt in reſpect of God, ſhe ſhall be praiſed for [Pg 20] One of his Excellent [199], Hidden Ones [200]: for one of his Iewels, which hee will make vp [201]: for His Daughter [202], His Siſter [203], His Mother [204], His Spouſe [205], His Loue [206], His Doue [207], His Faire [208] one, as Faire as the Moone, as Pure as the Sun [209]: as the Moone by inherent, and as the Sun, by imputed Righteouſneſſe. To her Huſband ſhe ſhall bee commended, as the Louing Hinde and pleaſant Roe [210], the Deſire of his eyes [211]; An Helpe like vnto Himſelfe [212]; His Companion [213]; for A Pillar of reſt [214], ſo that He ſhall haue no need of ſpoile [215]; for a Good Portion [216], a ſpeciall Fauour [217] and Gift of the Lord [218]; a Double Grace [219], Doubling the number of his Daies [220], Fatting his bones [221], and making him knowne in the Gates, when he ſitteth among the Elders of the Land [222]: for a Tower againſt Death vnto him [223]: A greater Bleſſing vnto him than either Houſe or Inheritance [224], Aboue children and the Building of a Citie to continue his Name [225], yea for a Crowne vnto her Huſband [226], not a Goldring on his finger; nor a chaine of Gold about his necke, nor a Brouch in his hat; but for a Crowne vpon his head (an Ornament more conſpicuous and eminent than the former, the Principall Enſigne of Princes [227]) gracing him that hath her, as much as a Crown doth Him that weareth it: ſo that there is none aboue her, that feareth the Lord [228], None greater than ſhe, not Great Men, nor Iudges, nor Potentates [229]: Her Grace is aboue Gold [230]. Her Price is farre aboue Rubies [231]. Her Continent minde cannot be valewed [232], and by reaſon of Her, her Huſband [Pg 21] is a Bleſſed Man [233], Not like other men [234].

# FOOTNOTES:

[189] ... *Nihil in illâ laudabo, nisi quod proprū est. S. Ierom ad Princip.*
And so of *Paula* he saith. *Nihil laudabimus nisi quod proprium est & de
puriſſimo sanctæ mentis fonte profertur. Id. ep. ad Euſtoch. Nam cum
omnia opera sua laudauerit Deus, cœlum, terram &c. vbi ad Hominē
vētum est, solus non videtur esse laudatus propter quem omnia generata
sūt. Quæ igitur cauſa est, nisi fortè ea, quia alia in ſpecie sunt, Homo in
occulto? quia aliorum Gratia foris, huius intus est. Aliorum in Natiuitate,
huius in Corde. — Ideo ergò homo non antè laudatur, quia non in forenſi
pelle, sed in interiore Homine antè probandus, sic prædicandus est. S. Ambros. Inſtit. Virg. cap. 3. tom. 1.*

[190] *2 Ioh. 1. 1. Hebr. 13. 1. Epheſ. 5. 25.*

[191] *1 Theſſ. 5. 13.*

[192] *Mark. 14. 9. Pſal. 112. 6.*

[193] *Gen. 23. 2. Ioh. 11. 33, 35. 1 King. 14. 13. 1 Theſ. 4. 13. Eccleſ.
22. 11, 12 & 38. 16, 17.*

[194] *Act. 8. 2. 2 Chron. 32. 33.*

[195] *Iam. 5. 10. Hebr. 12. 1. & 13. 7. 1 Cor. 11. 1.*

[196] *1 Sam. 2. 30. Deut. 26. 19. Ioh. 12. 26. Eſai. 8. 13. Timor Hominis, Dei Honor est. Tert. de Pœnit. c. 7*

[197] *Tho. Aquin. 22. q. 103. a. 1. ad 3.*

[198] *Pſal. 12. 6.*

[199] *Pſal. 16. 3.*

[200] *Pſal. 83. 3.*

[201] *Mal. 3. 17.*

[202] *2 Cor. 6. 18,*

[203] *Cant. 4. 9.*

[204] *Matth. 12. 50.*

[205] *Hoſ. 2. 19.*

[206] *Cant. 2. 10.*

[207] *Cant. 2. 14.*

[208] *Cant. 2. 13.*

[209] *Cant. 6. 10.*

[210] *Prou. 5. 19.*

[211] *Ezek. 24. 16. Ecclef. 36. 22.*

[212] *Gen. 2. 18. Ecclef. 36. 24.*

[213] *Mal. 2. 14.*

[214] *Ecclef. 36. 24.*

[215] *Prou. 31. 11.*

[216] *Ecclef. 26. 3, 23.*

[217] *Prou. 18. 22.*

[218] *Ecclef. 26. 14.*

[219] *Ecclef. 26. 15.*

[220] *Ecclef. 26. 1.*

[221] *Ecclef. 26. 13.*

[222] *Prou. 31. 23.*

[223] *Ecclef. 26. 22.*

[224] *Prou. 19. 14.*

[225] *Ecclef. 40. 19.*

[226] *Prou. 12. 4. Non annulus, non torques aureus, non monile, fed Corona. Cartw. in Prou.*

[227] *Pfal. 21. 3. Efth. 2. 17*

[228] *Ecclef. 25. 10.*

[229] *Ecclef. 10. 24.*

[230] *Ecclef. 7. 19.*

[231] *Prou. 31. 10.*

[232] *Ecclef. 26. 14. 15.*

To Her Children fhee fhall be Commended; becaufe by her they haue a place of Refuge [235]; by Her they haue good meanes to bring and continue true Honour vpon them [236], and if They (the Fruit) be a great Bleffing [237] (as it is to haue Iffue by fuch a One) what is the Root that beareth it [238]?

But I muft haften: How fhall fhe be Praifed in refpect of her Parents? euen as *Rachel* [239] for doing feruice to them as to her Mafters (the true propertie of one that *feareth the Lord* [240].) In refpect of her kindred by mariage, as *Ruth*, louing them [241], Dealing kindly with them [242], and Cleauing vnto them [243]. And in refpect of her kindred by bloud, as *Efther*, who did the Commandement of *Mordecay* when fhe was a Queene, like as when fhe was brought vp with Him [244], who was exceedingly grieued at his Griefe [245], and procured the Enlargement and Deliuerance of her kindred with her *Feafts* [246], her *Teares* [247], and the Hazard of her *Life* [248].

In regard of her Seruants alfo, fhe fhall be commended becaufe fhe Buildeth her Houfe [249]: *Shee is like the Merchants fhip, She fetcheth her food from farre* [250], *She giueth meat to her Houfhold* [251], *She cloatheth them all with Scarlet* [252], *and Shee looketh fo well to their waies* [253], that *As the Sunne when it arifeth in the high Heauen; So is her beautie in the Ordering of her Houfe* [254].

Laftly, becaufe all the Effentiall Glory and Faireneffe, which is to bee found in the whole Church, *The Woman cloathed with the Sunne* [255], as [Pg 22] that of Iuftification & Sanctification &c. belongs to euery Member of the Church [256], and côfequently to euery *Woman fearing the Lord*, therefore to Gods people fhe fhall be commended, as one of the Hands of the Church *dropping with fweet fmelling Mirrhe* [257]: as the *Curtaines of Salomon* [258]; *As a Lilly among thornes* [259]; *A Garden inclofed: A Spring fhut vp. A Fountain fealed* [260].

# FOOTNOTES:

[233] *Ecclef. 26. 1.*

[234] *Ecclef. 36. 23. Sine Muliere igitur Homo non habet Laudem, in Muliere prædicatur, &c. S. Ambros. Inftit. Virg. cap. 3. tom. 1.*

[235] *Prou. 14. 26. & 11. 22.*

[236] *Deut. 5. 29. Pfal. 112. 2.*

[237] *Pfal. 127. 3.*

[238] *Pfal. 128. 3.*

[239] *Gen. 29. 9.*

[240] *Ecclef. 3. 7.*

[241] *Ruth. 4. 15.*

[242] *Ruth. 1. 8.*

[243] *Ruth. 1. 14. & c. 2. 11*

[244] *Efth. 2. 20.*

[245] *Efth. 4. 4.*

[246] *Efth. 4. 16.*

[247] *Efth. 8. 3.*

[248] *Efth. 4. 11, 16.*

[249] *Prou. 14. 1.*

[250] *Prou. 31. 14.*

[251] *Prou. 31. 15.*

[252] *Prou. 31. 21.*

[253] *Prou. 31. 27.*

[254] *Ecclef. 26. 16.*

[255] *Reuel. 12. 1.*

But when fhall fhee haue all this Praife and of whom? Not by and by, nor of Euery one [261], for Praife is not comely in the mouth of euery one, of euery fcoffing *Ifhmael.*

II.

*When ſhe ſhall be Praiſed.*

But firſt of the Time.

Many when they heare a Promiſe (and a Promiſe I told you at firſt, this is) thinke to haue it by and by; but they marke not, that a Promiſe and the Fruition of it is not all at once. It muſt be waited for [262], eſpecially this Promiſe of Praiſe: *Vntill the Lord come* (as the Apoſtles limit the Time) *and then*, at his Appearing, *ſhe ſhall haue praiſe of God* [263]. *Then at his Appearing* [264], *Her Faith ſhall be found vnto Praiſe and Honour, and Glory.* Therefore in the mean while, beſt for her to *Feare the Lord*, and ſo be praiſe-worthy, than to be praiſed for the preſent.

1. Not only becauſe it is ſafeſt praiſing Her as a Maſter of a ſhip is (ſaith S. *Ambroſe* [265]) when ſhe [Pg 23] is ſafely arriued in the Hauen, paſt all danger of ſhipwracke: or growing more proud by her praiſe (which many Liuing doe) as *Herod* for one [266], and that Philoſopher for another, whoſe ſoule being before no bigger than a mans finger, became ſo puft vp and ſwolne with others commending him, that (as *Arrianus* reports) it grew greater than two Cubits [267].

# FOOTNOTES:

[256] *Gal. 3. 28. Ephef. 4. 15.16. Cant. 2. 10. – Cum ipfos cogitatis amantes, non virum & Fœminam, fed verbum &c. Animam fentiatis, oportet. Et fi Chriftum & Ecclefiam dixero, idem eft, nifi quod Ecclefiæ nomine non vna Anima, fed multarum vnitas, vel potius vnanimitas defignatur. S. Bern. ferm. 61. in Cant.*

[257] *Cant. 5. 5.*

[258] *Cant. 1. 5.*

[259] *Cant. 2. 2.*

[260] *Cant. 4. 12.*

[261] *Luk. 6. 26. Ecclef. 15. 9.*

[262] *Efay 28. 16. 30. 18. 40. 31. 64. 4. Heb. 10. 36, 37, 38. Hab. 2. 3, 4.*

[263] *1 Cor. 4. 5.*

[264] *1 Pet. 1. 7. Et nos ergò nō a nobis laudem exigamus, nec præripiamus iudicium Dei & præueniamus fententiam iudicis, fed fuo Tempori, fuo Iudici refervemus. S. Ambros. in Luc. l. 8. c. 17. tom. 5. 2 Tim. 2. 5. Ecclef. 11. 27.28.*

[265] *Nam fi laudari antè Gubernator non poteft quam in portum nauem deduxerit: quomodò laudabis Hominē priuf quàm in ftationem mortis fuccefferit? S. Ambr. de Bono Mort. c. 8. tom. 4. Meritò ergò differtur, vt fequatur fœnerata eius Laudatio, cuius dilatio non dispendium; fed incrementum eft … Et ideo luudutio eius non in exordio; fed in fine eft. Nemo enim nifi legitimè certauerit, coronabitur. Ideoq, fapiens tibi dicit: Antè mortem non laudes hominem quemquam. Ratio. Quia in fine hominis nudantur opera eius. Id. Inftit. Virg. c. 3. tom. 1.*

2. Nor only becaufe actuall praife is in the lips of the praifer, and fo a wicked woman may be praifed, and yet not be worthy of it, and a godly woman may be praife-worthy, and yet not haue it, whereas praife-worthineffe is euer in the partie to be praifed, and feweft (you know) haue this worth; but many haue praife without it, therefore praife-worthineffe is the Nobler Grace of the two, and confequently beft for a Woman to be worthy of praife, though fhe be not praifed for the prefent.

3. But one of the chiefeſt Reaſons is this; becauſe indeed all our earthly praiſe is *Laudatur*, that is, for the preſent; but continueth not. Is, but ſhall not be. Sometimes a godly woman is commended, and ſometimes ſhe is not. As S. *Paul* praiſed the *Corinthians* [268], *Now I praiſe you Brethren*, and by and by he ſaith: *Shall I praiſe you in this? I praiſe you not*: whereas This praiſe here promiſed ſo Is, that it *ſhall be* ſtill, and that cannot be in this Tranſitory world; but in Heauen, where Her praiſe that feareth the Lord for euer, endureth for euer: *Laudabitur, She ſhall be praiſed.*

III.
*Of whom ſhee ſhal be praiſed.*

The beſt Time then for commending Her is yet to come, and that from Him who can beſt doe it; [Pg 24] But I muſt tell you firſt, this Time ſhould neuer come, could the ſcoffing *Iſhmaels* of our daies be heard railing vpon, ieſting at, belying and ſlandering Her and Him *that feareth the Lord*. It was euer their Deuilliſh propertie [269] with many diſgracefull cenſures to dimme the glory of the children of Light, ſpitefully to aggrauate their tender frailties, rather than to commend their vnreproueable Graces. So of old they ſcourged the Primitiue Chriſtians with their viperous, virulent tongues [270]; but as Saint *Ierome* thanks God that He was counted worthy to be hated of the world [271]; ſo ſhould euery good man and woman, not much trouble themſelues for the vniuſt cenſures and diſconceits of witleſſe and worthleſſe prophaneneſſe; but rather (as *Paulinus* [272] exhorts) haue more regard to their good name, leſt any ſparkle or appearance of euill truly proceed from them, whereby any flame of euill report may be kindled, and ſo to liue, that none may ſpeake euill of them without lying. For maugre the malice of all Senſualiſts, the Time will come, when euery man and woman that feareth God, ſhall haue praiſe of God [273], 1 Cor. 4. which is the beſt praiſe, when all is done [274], 2 Cor. 10. Yea (Beloued) that you may not count *the Lord ſlacke* concerning his promiſe [275], Saint *Iames* tells you, This *comming of the Lord draweth neere* [276]: *Behold the Iudge ſtandeth at the doore, He is readie to iudge the Quicke and the Dead* (ſaith Saint *Peter* [277]) readie to commend them, whom the world hath condemned; and to condemne them, whom worldlings haue commended: readie to reueale vnto the [Pg 25] whole world the good workes of the godly, *Honorifico pietatis testimonio,* with an honourable approbation of their bleſſed godlineſſe; & alſo to reueale vnto the whole world the wicked Deeds of the vngodly, *Manifesto impietatis vituperio*, with a publike, and open, vncontrouleable Diſcommendation of their curſed wickedneſſe [278]: yea the Iudge is ready to turne *Laudabitur* into *Laudatur*, her praiſe worthineſſe that feareth Him for euer, into euerlaſting Praiſe; ſo that ſhould her Huſband and Children faile to praiſe Her, which yet they do not, for they commend Her in the 29. verſe of this Chapter, ſaying: *Many daughters haue done vertuouſly; but thou excellest them all* [279]: or ſhould the Godly ceaſe to praiſe Her, which they will neuer do either here or in Hcauen [280]. Here Her remembrance is ſo ſweet in all their mouthes, that they ſay: [281] Let her Memory be bleſſed: *Let her bones flouriſh out of her place*; and *Let the name of Her that was honoured be continued vpon her Children* [282]: or ſhould Her owne workes giue ouer praiſing Her in the Gates, which they are forbidden to doe, verſ. 31. of this Chapter; yet God himſelfe will haue *Her workes follow her to Heauen* [283], and *Accepting of her* [284], and *Them, by Chriſt Ieſus* [285], *Hee himſelfe will praiſe Her, that hath made Him Her Feare* [286], *Her praiſe* [287], ſaying: *Well done thou good and faithfull ſeruant, thou hast beene faithfull ouer a few things, I will make thee ruler ouer many things, Enter thou into the ioy of thy Lord* [288]. Where it is beſt to leaue Her, euen with her Lord, taking more ioy (as a Schoole-man teachcth truly) in praiſing Him, than in contemplating her [Pg 26] owne praiſe, in Glorifying God, than in her owne Glorification [289].

# FOOTNOTES:

[266] *Act. 12. 21.*

[267] *Arrian. Epict. l. 3. c. 2.*

[268] *1 Cor. 11. 1, 22*

[269] *2 Kings 9. 11. Act. 24. 5. & 26. 24. Neh. 6. 13.*

[270] *Tert. Apolog. c. 7. &c. Arnob. aduerſ. Gent. M. Fælix in Octau.*

[271] *Gratias ago Deo meo, quod dignus ſum, quem mundus oderit. S. Ierom. Aſellæ.*

[272] *Epheſ. 5. 15. Phil. 4. 8, 9. 2 Cor. 8. 20. 1 Pet. 2. 12. Heb. 11. 39. Eccl. 41. 12. – Nec ex nobis ſcintilla procedat, per quam aduerſus nos ſiniſtræ famæ flamma confletur – Nos id agamus, vt malè de nobis nemo loqui, abſque Mendacio poſſit. Paulin. epiſt. ad Celant.*

[273] *1 Cor. 4. 5.*

[274] *2 Cor. 10. 18. Iob. 12. 43.*

[275] *2 Pet. 3. 9.*

[276] *Iam. 5. 8, 9.*

[277] *1 Pet. 4. 5.*

[278] *Mat. 25. 34, 41.*

[279] *Prou. 31. 28, 29.*

[280] *Cant. 6. 9.*

[281] *Ecclef. 39. 10. Ecclef. 44. 15. Ecclef. 49. 1.*

[282] *Ecclef. 46. 11, 12.*

[283] *Reuel. 4. 13.*

[284] *Gen. 4. 4. Act. 10. 35. 1 Pet. 2. 5.*

[285] *Hebr. 13. 15.*

[286] *Eſai. 8. 13.*

[287] *Deut. 10. 21.*

[288] *Matth. 25. 21.*

But though we haue brought a Godly Woman where fhe would be, to Heauenly Praife, and Honour, and Glory, and found them by Gods free fauour in Chrift giuen vnto Her; yet who is fuch a Woman? We haue not found Her yet; and why not yet? Becaufe among other reafons, as Saint *Ierom* was afraid to entreat of the Death of that Venerable Matron *Paula* [290]; fo am I to fpeake of the Deceafe of this Honourable Lady. Therefore giue me leaue (beloued) to deferre the vncomfortable Paffions of her Death, vntill I be a little better heartened by relating fome of the laudable actions of her Life.

*Application. The Lady deceafed. Mulier Timēs Dominum.*

For the fubiect then of my Text, I dare fay, in regard of the Defcription thereof, your owne confciences haue made the Application, and doe witneffe for Her, that She was *A Woman fearing the Lord*. A Woman indeed, & fo the *Weaker Veffell* [291], yet neuertheleffe Honour to be giuen Her in that refpect; but rather the more (as Saint *Peters* inference will allow) becaufe though fhee had *This Treafure of the Feare of the Lord in an Earthen and in a Weaker Veffell* [292], yet Gods ftrength was made perfect in her Weakneffe. And it is S. *Ieroms* rule [293], you fhould iudge of Vertues, *Non Sexa, fed Animo*: Not by the Sex, but by the Minde and conftant purpofe of a Regenerate Heart: This makes the Difference of force in the feruice of Chrift, not either Male or Female.

Suruey then (if you pleafe) as briefly as you wil, [Pg 27] the feuerall workings of Her Godly Feare.

# FOOTNOTES:

[289] *Perfecta Die laudatio magis animā perficit, quàm Dei fruitio, quia magis lætatur in Gloriâ & plus gaudebit de Dei gloriâ & honore, quàm de ſuâ Glorificatione, & plus iocundabitur in laudando Dominū, quàm in conſiderādo proprium bonū. Bonau. l. 3. d. 1. q. 1, p. 66. A ſelm. Proſolog. c. 15. & 16.*

[290] *Quid agimus anima? cur ad mortem eius venire formidas? – S. Ier. Epitaph. Paulæ. Epiſt. ad Principiam. Gal. 3. 28.*

[291] *1 Pet. 3. 7.*

[292] *Eſai. 33. 6. 2 Cor. 4. 7.*

[293] *– Non conſiderantes Holdam & Annam ac Debboram, viris tacētibus prophetaſſe, & in ſeruitute Chriſti nequaquam differentiam Sexuum valere; ſed Mentium. S. Ierom. Euſtoch.*

*The workings of Godly feare in regard of Her: Husbād: Children.*

Firſt to Her Head, her Subiection and Helpfulneſſe like that of Saint *Auguſtines* Mother to his Father [294].

To Her Children, her tendereſt Affection and Sollicitouſneſſe to plant *the feare of the Lord* in their hearts, to fit them with worthy Matches out of Religious Families, to adorne her onely Sonne with the richeſt endowments of Grace and Learning: Witneſſe her Letters to that Learned Profeſſour [295] in our famous Vniuerſitie, worthy to be kept as a Monument of her truly Noble ſpirit and Godly Deſire (like that of *Gregory Nazianzen's* Siſter) to haue the fruit of her Body become the fruit of the Spirit [296].

*Parents.*

To Her Parents, ſhee was another *Rachel*, another *Marcella* [297].

*Kindred.*

To Her Kindred by mariage another *Ruth*, and to them by bloud another *Heſter*.

*Seruants.*

To Her Seruants, ſhee was bountifull in their Health; compaſſionate (as *Fabiola* [298]) in their Sickneſſe, either of Minde or of Body, prouiding for them (like the Centurion) both ſpirituall and corporall Phyſicke.

*Religious Deportmēt to all.*

To All, Her whole Deportment was ſo Louely, ſo ſweet, what *by the law of kindneſſe in her tongue* [299], Salutations, Gifts, Almes-Deeds, Viſitations, Inuitations, and by other offices of courteſies and Hoſpitalities, that Her Amiable Behauiour was a powerfull Meanes, an attractiue Load-ſtone to draw vnto Her the hearts and loues of as many as knew Her, yea as but heard of Her.

*Eſpecially vn-vnto Gods people.* [Pg 28]

But vnto Gods children ſhe euer only afforded the deareſt pangs, the higheſt Degree of her kindeſt Affection [300]: Their company ſhe moſt loued, and they Hers. Not ſo much in regard of Her fauour towards them, which was great; but chiefly by reaſon of that ſpiritual Helpe and refreſhment, which they might get by conuerſing with Her in the choiceſt paſſages of Sanctification. For ſhee had the Art to vphold holy conferences about perplexities of conſcience, Relapſes into ſin, and Remedies againſt the ſame: Shee had the skill to beget many ioyfull Meditations of mortifying Grace and euerlaſting Glory: She had the Zeale to nouriſh Heauenly mindedneſſe, boldneſſe in the waies, and cheerefulneſſe in the exerciſes of Religion and Deuotion.

# FOOTNOTES:

[294] *S. Aug. Confeſſ. lib. 9. cap. 9.*

[295] Doct. *Prideaux* Rector of Exceter College in *Oxford.*

[296] *Greg. Nazian. in Laudem Gorgon. Orat. 25.*

[297] *S. Ier. ad Princip. Nuſquam ſine Matre &c. –*

[298] *Id. Epitaph. Fabiola.*

[299] *Prou. 31. 26.*

*Conſtant vſe of the Meanes of Saluation.*

Touching Her ſubmiſſion to the Meanes of Saluation: O what delight ſhee tooke here and in *London*, to heare conſcionable and ſearching Sermons! It was Her onely Pleaſure in that Citie (as ſhe profeſſed) to frequent them there; yea what Griefe was it vnto Her (as it was vnto Saint *Ambroſe*) to heare of the Death of any of Gods zealous Miniſters [301]?

And ſhould I be ſilent, yet Her Oratory in her houſe hereby, this Church too (a part whereof her Zeale, together with her Honourable Huſbands Loue to Gods Houſe newly erected) that Cloſſet alſo of Hers in *Truro*, yea euery place almoſt would ſpeake aloud of her conſtant reading, hearing, meditating on the Word, ſolemne Humiliations, ſolitary conferences with her God, feruent [Pg 29] prayers and eiaculations, which (as the ſweeteſt incenſe) ſhee euer and anon ſent vp to the Throne of Grace for the pardon of her ſinnes, the fauour of God, the ſpirituall Good of her Deareſt Huſband, Children, and Gods Church.

# FOOTNOTES:

[300] *Pſal. 16. 3. Pſal. 119. 63, 79. Gal. 6. 10. 1 Pet. 2. 17. Coloſſ. 1. 4.*

[301] *Paulin. in Vitâ D. Ambroſ.*

*Vnfained Reſolution to mortifie her moſt preuailing Sinne.*

But adde vnto all theſe, another more ſpeciall, eſſentiall, and ſuperiour working of Her Godly Feare, and that was Her continuall Combating againſt all ſinne, euen Her moſt commanding ſin whatſoeuer that was [302]. For there was a time to my knowledge, when after the preaching vnto Her of the power and efficacie of Gods promiſes, and of Chriſts Death and Reſurrection, for the mortifying and maſtering of any boſome and beloued ſinne, you might eaſily ſee in Her, how willingly ſhe yeelded vnto the Sanctifying worke of the Holy Ghoſt for the Ouer-comming of her ſtrongeſt corruptions, how heauily ſhee was diſpleaſed with relapſes into ſmaller offences of daily incurſion againſt the generall and conſtant purpoſe [303] of her heart not to ſinne in anything; how faithfully ſhe reſted vpon thoſe ſweeteſt [304] promiſes of God (which ſhe confeſſed ſhe had not erſt ſo well weighed) for the mortifying of ſpeciall infirmities, and how vnfainedly ſhee reſolued to ſet her Faith on worke, to draw not onely aſſurance of pardon from the Merit of Chriſts Death and Reſurrection; but alſo that Power and efficacie which is in them, to *Die to Sinne, and Liue to Righteouſneſſe.* [305] [Pg 30]

# FOOTNOTES:

[302] *Pſal. 18. 23. Rom. 7. 21, 22, 23, 24.*

[303] *Pſal. 119. 6, 8. Act. 11. 23.*

[304] *Mic. 7. 18. 1 Ioh. 1. 9. Rom. 6. 14. Ez. 36. 25. 2 Cor. 12. 7, 9.*

[305] *Rom. 6. 4, 5, &c. Vis, inquam, illa Chriſti mortis nobis communicatur, vt per hāc Chriſtivim moriamur peccato, ſicut Chriſtus peccato ſemel mortitus eſt, id eſt, non vt peccatum nobis non imputitur, (id enim ad Iuſtiſicationem pertinct) ſed vt peccati vis iam non ſit in nobis efficax, immo verò contrà freti vi illâ Chriſti, cui per Spiritum Sanctum coniuncti ſumus, peccatum occidamus. — piſtiemò quia non ſatis eſt nō peccare; ſed etiam benè agere oportet, eadem vis illa Chriſti, quâ victor peccati et mortis in carne noſtrâ viuere cœpit Deo — nobiſcum communicata facit vt &c. Beza epiſt. Theolog. 45. p. 211.*

This was the Life of this Elect Lady fearing the Lord, and therefore ſhe hath right and intereſt to all thoſe Honourable Attributes of Praiſe, which you heard euen now God himſelfe giue her in His owne words.

*Bountie to the Poore.*

But O my Soule what doſt thou? Why art thou yet afraid to come to her Death? as if while I held my peace and were buſied in Her Praiſes, Her Death could be deferred? Alâs it could not by all the Meanes that were vſed. For *No man* (ſaith the Preacher) *hath power ouer the ſpirit to retuine the ſpirit* [306]. Then ſpeake of her Death I muſt, and yet (to make vſe of S. *Ierom's* words in a like caſe) *Quis poſſit ſiccis oculis Paulam narrare morientem [307]?* Who can relate the Death of the Lady *Frances Roberts* without ſhedding ſome Teares of Compaſſion, of Deuotion, yea and of Compunction too [308]? Shee deſerues ſome Teares from vs (Beloued) as well as from the Poore, weeping now and ſhewing the Coats and garments which this *Dorcas* made for them, while ſhe was with them [309].

*Thākfulneſſe for Deliuerance from the Plague.*

But to ſtop the current of them a little longer. Begin we with Gods mercifull preſeruation of Her in *London* from the noyſome Peſtilence; becauſe ſhe acknowledged it (as was meet) with humble Thankful-

neſſe [310]. And then remember, that vpon Her returne home, being
ſummoned by Sickneſſe, by and by ſhe ſet her *Houſe in order*, like
*Hezekiah*; She ſpake to the Hearts of Her Children, Friends, and Seruants, that were then about Her (like *Iacob*) by putting them in
remembrance of Her Departure and their Duties: She hungered and
thirſted [Pg 31] after the Body and Bloud of Her Deareſt Sauiour,
which ſhee receiued with Due Examination [311] of Her Knowledge;
Faith; Loue and Repentance, with reuerent Geſture, heartie Thank-
fulneſſe, deuout Attention, and very Fruitfully to the greater
ſtrengthning and refreſhing of Her Soule then trauelling for the
other Life.

# FOOTNOTES:

[306] *Eccleſ. 8. 8.*

[307] *S. Ierom. Euſtoch. Epitaph. Paul.*

[308] *Neq, parū diſtat inter has lachrymas Deuotionis & ætatis vtiq, iam virilis, atque eas quas primæus ætas inter infantiæ vagit' emiſit, lachrymas vtiq, pœnitentiæ & confeſſionis. Veruntamen longè amplius vtriſque procèdunt aliæ quædā lachrymæ, quibus in funditur ſapor vini. Illas enim lachrymas verè in vinū mutari dixerim, quæ Fraternæ Compaſſionis affectu in feruore prodeūt charitatis, pro qua etiā ad horam tui ipſius immemor eſſe, ſobria quadā ebrietate videris. S. Bern. in Epiph. Dom. Serm. 3.*

[309] *Act. 9. 36.*

[310] *Pſal. 91. 7. Pſal. 50. 15. Pſal. 33. 1.*

*Worthy receiving the Sacrament.*

And now (Beloued) that ſhe lieth on the bed of Languiſhing, we muſt not be auſtere in reprehending euery Infirmity; but Pitifull in conſidering the tender frailtie of it.

*Paſſionatneſſe by reaſon of Spiritual and Bodily Diſtĕper.*

For what though ſhee were (as Sicke folke are commonly [312]) more Paſſionate than others, yea than Her ſelfe in Her health, yet if God iudgeth not according to the ſtrange Effects and Symptoms of Her ſickneſſe, not according to the ſhort moment and violent paſſions of Her Death; but according to the holy Actions of Her Health, the former Affections of Her Heart, and the Generall Courſe of Her Life [313]; then it is our Dutie, not ſeuerely to cenſure her paſſionateneſſe, who by reaſon of the parching Feauer of the Spirit, as well as of the Body, was diſquieted in her Imagination (as the Phyſitian of the body could diſcerne) though not in her Memory. Conſider therefore O Man (as that excellent Phyſitian of the Soule aduiſeth thee [314]) if thou canſt beare with a fraile Body, that thou muſt much more beare with a fraile Minde and Body too. Conſider alſo O Man, that this her Pettiſhneſſe did more wound her to the heart, than any iniury thou couldſt preſſe her with. Neither doe I ſpeake this to nouriſh paſſion [Pg 32] in any, or to proue her Anger to be Sinleſſe [315]; but to be a leſſe Sinne, becauſe her Spirituall and Bodi-

ly Diſtemper was ſo great, or rather becauſe her Faith quenched the
flame of this fiery paſſion in Chriſts Bloud, reſolued and melted her
heart into many penitent Teares afterwards. Oh, ſaid ſhe to me,
(preſſing her with *Dauids* example, *Pſal. 131.*) In my Health I could
digeſt any iniury, and deemed it baſe and vngodly, not to be able to
doe ſo; but now (I know not how) me thinkes I am ouer-tender in
bearing them. I am impatient indeed, and then I weepe for my impatiencie. For I know (as ſhe her ſelfe vrged) *The wrath of Man doth
not accompliſh the Righteouſneſſe of God* [316].

# FOOTNOTES:

[311] *1 Cor. 1. 28.*

[312] [Greek: Dusareston hoi nosountes aporias hupo] *Eurip. Or-*
*est.*

[313] M^r. *Greenham.* 1. Treat. for Afflict. Confc. fol. III. part 2.

[314] *Id. Of Death, fol. 9. part 2.*

*Repentance for the fame.*

Thus fhee was Angrie with her felfe for being Angrie with others,
and then (according to Saint *Ambrofes* rule) it ceafed towards them
before the Sunne went down [317]; and was not this Holy Reuenge
on her felfe a true fruit of Euangelicall Repentance? *2 Cor. 7. 11.*

*Her Agonie.*

But aye me! me thinkes I now heare her groaning vunder the
dolefull pangs of Death, vnder thofe pangs of which fhee had fore-
told faying: I fhall fuffer much more ere I goe hence. And can any
haue the heart to heare her groaning pangs, without renting his
owne heart from his darling pleafure? without lamenting his owne
finnes, which vnleffe he forfake betimes, will bring him to euerlaft-
ing Burnings [318]? or without learning to compaffionate euery
weake one, to affift any one yeelding vp the Ghoft, becaufe (as Saint
*Ambrofe* giues the reafon [319]) the holy Peophet *Iob* defired [Pg 33]
the Bleffing of one, that lyes a Dying: *Benedictio morituri, in me veniat:*
*Let the bleffing of him that is readie to die, come vpon me!*

# FOOTNOTES:

[315] *Vitemus ergò aut temperemus iracūdiam: ne fit eius aut in Laudi-bus exceptio, aut in vitijs exaggeratio. S. Ambr. Off. lib. 1. cap. 21.*

[316] *Iam. 1. 20. Pfalm. 4. 4.*

[317] *Ephef. 4. 26. Vel certè fic: Si irafcimini, vobis irafcimini, quia commoti eftis, & non peccabitis. Qui enim fibi irafcitur, quia citò cōmotus eft, definit irafci alteri. Id. ibid.*

[318] *Ezek. 18. 13, 30.*

[319] *– Si quem viderimus pauperē moriturum, fumptu iuvemus, & dicat vnufquifq, noftrûm: Benedictio morituri in me veniat: Si quē viderimus debilem, non deferamus, fi quem in extremis pofitum, non relinquam.* S. *Ambrof. de Bono Mort. cap. 8. tom. 4.*

*Deuotion at Her Death.*

Let vs then, not yet, leaue this Departing Saint. For in the midft of this her Agonie, after fhee had layen groaning many houres without any articulate or diftinct fpeech, yet vpon triall made of Her fenfe and memory by demanding of Her, whether fhe would haue prayers made for Her, fhe anfwered plainly. With all my heart, pray, pray. And then as *Gregory Nazianzen* [320] reports of his Father, that though He was daily, yea hourely, in great paine before his Death, yet He was euer ftill and quiet from paine, onely while Diuine Seruice was faying; fo this Deuout Lady forgetting (as it were) Her former Groanings, did liften attentiuely to the prayers that were made for Her, without fetching fo much as one fob during that time. And afterwards rehearfing diftinctly part of the Lords Prayer, you might heare Her, when S. *Stephens* Vifion and laft words [321] were read vnto Her, repeat very often thefe laft words of Her Sauiour [322]: *O Heauenly Father into thy hands I commend my fpirit.* Thus on a fudden I haue told you how fhe *Dyed in the Lord* [323], and is *with Chrift* [324].

And though we faw her afterwards mouing her lips; but heard not her Voice, no more than they that were at Saint *Ambrofes* Death did heare his Voice; but only faw his lips moue [325]; yet we muft not thinke *The Spirit of ftrength* [326], of *Prayer* and *Grace* [327], is then onely ſtrong, when we heare a Dying Saint pray, becauſe Chriſts Spirit cries in [Pg 34] Gods Children, *Abba, Father* [328], with Vnutterable Groanings [329] which we cannot heare, and therefore I doubt not, but this Elect Lady cried loudeſt in Gods eares, when we heard not her words; and why may we not thinke now, our ſinnes hindered vs from hearing them? I am ſure, heretofore ſhe hath ſpoken againe and againe many Heart-piercing ſpeeches to deterre from Sinne, and to allure to Holineſſe of Life. If ſhe be not hearkened to now, henceforth wee ſhall heare Her ſpeake no more. *I charge you therefore before God and the Lord Ieſus Chriſt, and the Elect Angells*: [330] you (I ſay) I charge whomſoeuer ſhee hath iuſtly reproued for any Sin, that you forſake thoſe Sins; and whomſoeuer ſhe hath zealouſly exhorted to holy Duties, that you performe thoſe holy Duties, for henceforth you ſhall heare Her ſpeake no more.

# FOOTNOTES:

[320] *Orat. 28. de Funere Patris. Tom. 2.*

[321] *Act. 7. 53, 56, 59.*

[322] *Luke 23. 46.*

[323] *Reuel. 14. 13.*

[324] *Phil. 1. 23.*

[325] *Paulin. in D. Ambroſ Vita.*

[326] *Eſai. 11. 2.*

[327] *Zach. 12. 10.*

*Concluſion. Sed quid ego te morer Frater? quid expectem? vt noſtra tecum cōmoriatur et quaſi conſepeliatur oratio? S. Ambr. de Obitu fratris. Tom. 3.*

But why ſhould I detaine thee (Honourable Lady) any longer? Or what doe you (Beloued) expect more? That our ſpeech alſo ſhould Die together with Hers, and (as it were) be Buried together with Hcr. O my Bleſſed Brethren, ſuffer neither this Godly Lady, nor Gods word to depart ſo diſhonourably from you.

I.
*Imitation of Her Vertues.*

Suffer not Her ſo to depart from you; but let her euer liue in your breaſts by Eſteeming Her very highly in loue for Her workes ſake, by Commemorating Gods Graces in Her; but aboue all by Imitating her Faith and Vertues [331]. Then you ſhall not need to grieue very much for Her Abſence [Pg 35] from you; becauſe ſhe is *with Chriſt, which is beſt of all* [332]; becauſe ſhe is *Taken away*, not from you; but *from the euill to come, Eſai. 57. 1.* From you ſhee is not Taken, but from ſeeing the plagues and miſeries of this wretched world, yea from ſeeing the future Deaths of you, Her Deareſt friends [333], for whom ſhe would haue wept full bitterly; but you haue greater Cauſe, if you will heare S. *Ambroſe* and S. *Ierome* comforting them-ſelues in a like caſe, to Reioyce [334] and to giue God thankes [335], that you Haue had Her, nay that you Haue Her, if ſo be you follow Her good example, and repreſent her to the life by your Godly Life.

# FOOTNOTES:

[328] *Gal. 4. 6.*

[329] *Rom. 8. 26.*

[330] *1 Tim. 5. 21.*

[331] *Ideò laude oris ad Hominem vtimur, vt alios apud quos laudatur, in bonam opinionem, & Reuerentiam, & Imitationem ipſius inducamus. Thom. Aquin. 22. q. 91.*

II.
*Practiſe of Gods word.*
III.
*Means to Godly Feare.*
IV.
*So Great a Feare as muſt feare vs from our Boſome Sinne.*

To conclude: I beſeech you all (Bleſſed Brethren) Suffer not the Word of God, which you haue heard this day, for want of the Feare of God, which is *The firmeſt foundation of Gods word* [336], to vaniſh into aire, into nothing, to rebound from your flintie hearts (as a ſhaft ſhot againſt a wall of Adamant [337];) but in Gods Name, Let the Sword of Gods Spirit ſunder euery one of our minion ſinnes from our boſomes: Let Gods pretious promiſe here of praiſing a *Woman that feareth the Lord*, feare vs from our ſtrongeſt corruptions. *Atq vtinam præconia fœminarum, imitarentur viri.* And I may well wiſh with Saint *Ierome*, that Men would emulate and imitate Women in their deſerued attributions [Pg 36] of Praiſe [338]. Laſtly, if you deſire to know, beſides this motiue of obtaining Heauenly praiſe, what other Meanes you ſhould vſe to get, keepe and increaſe ſuch a godly Feare in you, then conſider the examples of Gods dreadfull iudgements [339] on them, that Feare Him not, yea on Chriſt Ieſus Himſelfe purſued for our ſins [340] to the fulneſſe of Bitterneſſe by the iuſtice of God, conſider that firſt. Then remember your owne Deaths to haue them before you [341], remember your ſtrict Accounts to be made [342], remember the reſtleſſe Terrour of Conſcience [343], which followes the impenitent, and then or neuer you will *Feare the Lord Greatly*, as *Obadiah* and this Bleſſed Lady did. Be not deceiued (my Brethren) after all this Hearing, it is not a Little Feare will ſerue

the turne. For to Feare God but a little (as *Fulgentius* ſaith) is to contemne Him very much [344]. It muſt bee at leaſt ſo Great a Feare, as
muſt feare you from your Greateſt, your Sweeteſt Sinne whatſoeuer
that be, elſe if you Die in it [345] without Repentance (which God
forbid) your *Worme ſhall not die, neither ſhall your fire be quenched, and
you ſhall be*, not a praiſe, but *an Abhorring to all fleſh*, the laſt verſe of
the Prophet *Eſay* with *Iames* 2. 10. [346], and *Ezekiel.* 18. 10, 11, 13.

# FOOTNOTES:

[332] *Phil. 1. 23. — Et Chriſtum lædimus cùm euocatos quoſque ab illo quaſi miſerandos non æquanimitèr accipimus. Cupio, inquit Apoſtolus, recipi iam … Ergo votum ſi alios conſequutos impatientèr dolemus, ipſi conſequi nolumus. Tertul. de Patient. cap. 9. Temperet ſanè Dilecti Gaudiũ, mœſtitiam deſolatorum, & tolerabilius fiat nobis, quod Nobiſcum non eſt, quia cum Deo eſt. Ber. in Cant. ſer. 27.*

[333] *Non enim nobis ereptus es, ſed periculis. — raptus eſl ne totius orbis excidia, mundi finem, propinquorũ funera, &c. S. Ambroſ. de Obitu Fratru. fol. 17.*

[334] *Lætandum eſt enim magis, quòd talem fratrem habuerim, quàm dolendum, quòd fratrem amiſerim. Illud enim munus, hoc debitum eſt. Idem ibid. fol. 13.*

[335] *Non mæremus quod talem amiſimus, ſed gratias agimus, quòd habuimus, immo habemus. S. Ierom. Epitaph. Paulæ.*

[336] *Baſis quædam Verbi eſt Timor ſanctus. Sicut enim ſimulachrum aliquod in Baſi ſtatuitur — — ita verbum Dei in Timore Sancto melius ſtatuitur, fortiùs radicatur, hoc eſt, in pectore timentis Dominum — S. Ambros. in Pſal. 118. Serm. 5.*

[337] *Iam. 1. 22. Zach. 7. 12.*

[Pg 37]

[338] *S. Ierom. epiſt. ad Furiam.*

[339] *1 Cor. 10. 11. Reuel. 14. 7.*

[340] *Eſai. 57. 11. & 53. 5. Mat. 27. 46.*

[341] *Eccleſ. 3. 14. Iob 7. 1. Pſal. 39. 4. & 90. 12.*

[342] *2 Cor. 5. 10. Matth. 12. 36.*

[343] *Rom. 2. 15. Reu. 6. 16. Pſal. 18. 23. Prou. 8. 13.*

[344] *— Hunc ſi quis parum metuit, valde contemmi — B. Fulg. de Myſt. Mediat. ad Traſim. l.2. pag. 215.*

[345] *Si in ſolo vno peccato deceſſerit Homo, irreuocabilitèr mittitur in ignem æternum — Gerſon. 2. p. de Mendicit. Spirit. lit. D & H. part. 3.*

[346] *Ex parte enim Auerſionis dicit Iacobus qui offendit in vno factus eſt omnium reus, quia scilicet vno peccato peccando incurrit pœnæ reatum, ex hoc, quod contemnit Deum, ex cuius contemptu prouenit omnium peccatorū reatus. Aquin. 12. q. 73. a.1 ad fin. Peccatum enim remitti non poteſt, quam disi Voluntas peccato adheret. Idem. p. 3. q. 87. a. 1. c. & q. 86. a. 2. c. Vnde non poteſt eſſe vere pœnitens, qui de vno peccato pœnitet, & non de alio. Si enim diſpliceret ei illud peccatum, quia eſt contra Deum ſuper omnia dilectum — Sequeretur, quod de omnibus peccatis pœniteret. Id. q. 86. a. 3. c.*

V.
*Reaſons to feare the Lord.*
VI.
*Prayer for Godly Feare.*

*Knowing therefore* (as Saint *Paul* concludes [347]) *the terrour of the Lord, we perſwade you* (Bleſſed Brethren) *to feare God* Greatly, and to *Giue Glory vnto Him* [348]; then you *ſhall haue praiſe of Him*, then hee *will glorifie* you; and to ſay no more than this (with the Prophet *Ieremie* [349],) which will make the Fearleſſe Sinner inexcuſable: *Who would not feare thee O Lord, thou King of Nations, thou King of Saints?* 1. *For thou onely art Holy:* 2. *For all Nations ſhall come vnto thee, and worſhip thee:* 3. *For thy iudgements are made manifest* [350]: 4. *For there is none like vnto thee, that pardoneth Iniquitie, and paſſeth by the Tranſgreſſion of the remnant of thy Heritage* [351]? Who would not Feare Thee ſuch an *Almightie, All-ſeeing, Iuſt, Mercifull Lord God?* Put thy feare *therefore in our Hearts* (as thou haſt promiſed [352]) *that wee may neuer depart from thee;* but clinging inſeparably by a liuely faith, vnto the bleeding wounds of our Bleſſed Redeemer, may without all ſlauiſh Feare [353] of Death and Iudgement, Louingly [354] appeare before thy Iudgement-ſeat, and without deſperate *Crying to the mountains and rocks Fall on vs* [355], may ioyfully heare Thee ſay vnto vs: *Come ye Bleſſed of my Father, Inherit the Kingdome prepared for you from the foundation of the world* [356].

Which God grants vnto vs all, for the All-ſufficient Merits of his Deareſt Sonne, the Sweet Lord Ieſus: To whom with Himſelfe and the Holy Spirit be aſcribed *All Praiſe, Honour, Glory, Power, Dominion and Maieſtie, now and euer. Amen. Amen.*

FINIS.

# FOOTNOTES:

[347] *2 Cor. 5. 10, 11.*

[348] *Reuel. 14. 7.*

[349] *Ier. 10. 7.*

[350] *Reuel. 15. 4.*

[351] *Mic. 7. 18.*

[352] *Ier. 32. 39.*

[353] *Si enim amamus Chriſtum, vtiq aduentum eius deſiderare debemus. Peruerſum enim eſt, & neſcio vtrum verū, quem diligis, timere ne veniat, orare, Veniat regnū tuū, & timere, ne exaudiaris. Vnde autem timor? ... Quisquis ergò futurū iudicē times, præsentē cōscientiā tuā corrige. S. Aug. in Pſal. 147. tom 3.*

[354] *2 Tim. 4. 8.*

[355] *Reuel. 6. 16.*

[356] *Matth. 25. 34.*